REUNITED

by

JOHN G. FINDLAY

Author of

The Unbroken Melody of Life

PSYCHIC PRESS LTD.
144 HIGH HOLBORN, LONDON, W.C.1
1946

PREFACE.

THERE are millions of people living in the world to-day who have received definite proof that man survives the death of the physical body. The belief that there is another state of existence, into which we pass when our time on earth is over, is no longer merely a matter of faith or a pious hope. It no longer depends on speculation or tradition. It is a definitely proved scientific fact, and if only people were taught aright this fact would be known and understood by all.

Unfortunately, owing to prejudice and the objections raised by vested interests, the vast majority of people are totally ignorant of the kind of life we enter upon when death takes place. Many books have been written on the subject; many eminent men in various walks of life have investigated the matter and have publicly testified to their own experiences; but by far the largest volume of evidence for survival is to be found among ordinary men and women who neither write books nor speak on public platforms, and therefore have no means of making their knowledge available to the world at large.

The fact that we can communicate with our departed loved ones is by no means so fantastic or revolutionary as at first sight it appears. It may be condemned by those whose teaching on the subject has now been proved to be wrong. It may be suppressed by antiquated Acts of Parliament, still enforced to-day, which seek to prevent it from being demonstrated or talked about. It may be scoffed at by the ignorant. But none of these things can alter the fact that communication is not only possible but that it takes place in thousands of halls and homes throughout the world every day of the week, and that such communications are a constant source of comfort and consolation to those who mourn.

This book adds another stone to the cairn of evidence which has been, and is being, erected by those who have obtained definite proof that those whom they once thought were "dead" are still their constant, if unseen, companions. It has been written for one purpose only—to bring this truth to the knowledge of others, in the hope that their interest may be awakened and that they, too, may investigate for themselves this most important of all subjects.

JOHN G. FINDLAY.

TOUR,
   KILMAURS,
      AYRSHIRE,
         APRIL, 1946.

CONTENTS.

CHAPTER I.

A VITAL QUESTION.

SOME years ago the " Daily Mail " conducted an inquiry into what it termed " one of the greatest religious and social problems of the day." The subject of that inquiry was Spiritualism. Much has already been written both in favour of and against this controversial subject, and doubtless much will still be written in the future. But the fact that, in summing up its conclusions, the " Daily Mail " admitted that " no inquiry of this nature has ever before excited such widespread interest " plainly indicates that Spiritualism is not a subject which can lightly be dismissed as being of no importance, but that it is, in fact, one which is worthy of careful and thoughtful study.

" If it were possible," wrote the " Daily Mail " after the inquiry had ended, " to take a straight vote for or against Spiritualism from the letters sent in to us, there is no doubt that there would be a vast majority in favour." This conclusion, reached after a prolonged and impartial investigation, must give pause to those critics who so glibly affirm that Spiritualism is either fraud on the one hand or merely foolishness on the other, and whose qualifications for expressing any opinion on the subject are generally found to be virtually non-existent.

A great deal of prejudice has been created in the minds of many people by the mistaken idea that Spiritualism is some new-fangled form of belief which has crept in to take its place among numerous other "isms" of present-day thought. This is far from being the case. The name may be new, but what that name stands for is as old as the human race. Those who think that Spiritualism means nothing more than holding communication, more or less successfully, with those whom the world calls " dead," have a poor and altogether unworthy idea of the true meaning of the word. Communication with the Unseen World is nothing new. In olden times it was looked upon as a natural phenomenon, spoken and written about as a matter of everyday occurrence, not worthy of special mention.

It is only during modern times, when people's minds have been gradually drifting towards Materialism, that they have lost touch with those unseen spiritual forces which surround us. They have become oblivious to their existence. The average individual, who is frankly not specially interested in much beyond the day-to-day affairs of his life, has either given unthinking acceptance to the teaching of the Churches or has rejected that teaching and has been content to remain agnostic.

But in recent years this attitude has changed. Education—and in that comprehensive term I include, not only the school-room, but the stage, the cinema, free libraries and a host of other means by which knowledge can be acquired—has slowly but surely been forcing people to think for themselves. The old orthodox heaven of golden streets and pearly gates and the hell of fire and brimstone are no longer held before the frightened gaze of an ignorant world, much as a carrot is held before the nose of a donkey or a stick is applied to its hindquarters. To-day the pulpit is led by the pew and the pulpit has wisely seen the red flag and has changed its tune. But it still maintains that anything it may say on the subject of a future life is only a " belief." It still insists that its followers must live—and die—by faith alone. It overlooks the fact that, having been forced by public opinion to relinquish the old teaching of Heaven and Hell, an increasingly intelligent public may possibly not be prepared to accept from its lips any new teaching, without some justification for that teaching being produced for their inspection.

The public of to-day asks for proof, and that is just what our religious teachers will not give. I do not say they *cannot* give it. I know that many of them can. But they *won't.* An increasing number of clergy and ministers of all denominations are now visiting Spiritualist mediums and are becoming convinced of the possibility of communication between us and those who have passed on. But it is not in their interests to say so. A few have been bold enough to make open confession of their convictions, and have had to suffer in consequence. They have been forced to give up their charges and go out into the wilderness, pursued by the anathemas of their less honest brethren, who are either too timid to investigate themselves or too much in fear of the voice of Authority to say publicly what they know to be true.

And so, officially, from the viewpoint of religious teaching, Spiritualism is " taboo." Only those who have the temerity to free themselves from the shackles of orthodoxy and investigate the subject for themselves, know for a certainty that Truth is being suppressed and that belief has given place to Knowledge.

I must confess that the attitude of the Churches towards Spiritualism is difficult to understand. They have always taught that there is a life after death, crude and fantastic though that teaching may have been. Their whole scheme of " salvation " is centred round and based upon the creed that at some future date we are to be judged and assigned to the particular place in which we are to spend eternity. If there were no after-life there would be no need for religion. If this life were all, and death the end of our being, then let us eat, drink and be merry, for to-morrow we die. The race would then be to the strong, and the weak would merely be crushed out of existence a few short years sooner than their more fortunate fellow-beings.

But the belief in a life to come, and the hope or fear of what that life may consist of, has always been an incentive to the pious just as it has been a curb to the would-be sinner. And yet, when Spiritualism produces indisputable proofs which confirm the fact that there is an after-life, what reception does it receive from the official custodians of our spiritual welfare ?

One would have thought that the vital discovery that there definitely is an after-life would have been given a cordial welcome. One would have thought that it would have been seized upon with eagerness ; that our spiritual advisers would, so to speak, have climbed to the topmost pinnacles of their churches and broadcast it joyfully to their followers—" Come now ! we can now prove to you as a definite and scientifically demonstrated fact that which we have hitherto told you to believe by faith alone. We can now show you by practical experience, and beyond all shadow of doubt, that our teaching has been true."

That is what one would have expected, but we know that what actually happened was something very different.

Instead of being received with any show of kindliness, or even tolerance, Spiritualism has been abused and ridiculed by the very people to whom it should have made the greatest appeal. We have been called many hard names. Spiritualism has suffered the same fate as all new thought and every progressive reform, which has been introduced into the world by people who have been able to see a little further ahead than the rest.

Glance back for a moment over the history of our own country since the beginning of last century. What of the great pioneers and reformers who have arisen in our midst since then ? How did they fare, and how were they received by their fellows? Let us consider very briefly one or two outstanding examples.

In 1787, William Wilberforce set himself the great task of abolishing slavery within the British Empire. He soon found that he had other things besides slavery to contend with. He was violently opposed by those whom he had every right to expect would be his friends. Chief among his detractors were the bishops in the House of Lords, clergymen and professing " Christian " laymen, who had financial interests in the slave ships, and were willing that any form of cruelty should be practised on their fellow human beings so long as their pockets benefited thereby. Only after twenty years of patient and unremitting labour in the face of this opposition did he at last realise his dreams. He was then permitted to introduce a Bill into Parliament which, after prolonged discussion, at last received the Royal assent.

Much the same can be said of that great philanthropist of the 19th century, Anthony Ashley Cooper, 7th Earl of Shaftesbury. Although he undertook the work of reforming the Poor Law and of improving the lot of the factory workers, especially the children, soon after he entered Parliament in 1826, it was not until many years later that he succeeded in achieving the first of these objects. In his diary he writes despondently of " the opposition of the Evangelical party," and deplores how " in very few instances did the ministers of any religious denomination appear on the platform with me. At first not one, except the Rev. Mr. Bull, of Brierley, and even to the last very few, so indifferent were they, or so cowed by the overwhelming influence of the cotton lords." When writing of the bitter opposition in the House of Commons to his Ten Hours' Bill, he says " The more I think the more I am embarrassed and perplexed ; the Established Church on one side, the Dissenters on the other, seem to present insurmountable difficulties."

Charles Darwin was denounced from every pulpit in the land when he published his famous book, " The Origin of Species." The orthodox of his day coined the phrase, " I'd rather be descended from an angel than from a monkey." It sounds well, no doubt, but angels do not tolerate slavery or amass wealth by overworking young children. In fact, I imagine that even a monkey would not be so heartless as to treat its young like that !

James Simpson, the discoverer of chloroform, was similarly abused, on the grounds that pain and suffering were a legacy left to mankind by Adam and Eve, and that anything which tended to alleviate pain must therefore be contrary to the will of God.

These are but a few instances taken at random, but while the attitude of the Churches has remained unaltered, that of the people in general has moved with the times. And as times have changed, so the narrow-minded and intolerant opinions which were so common a generation ago have given place to a wider and more generous consideration of the views of others. No longer do Spiritualists have stones thrown through their windows, or gibes and insults hurled at them as they walk through the streets. The attitude of the public Press has also changed. The " Daily Mail " is by no means the only popular newspaper which has stimulated public interest in the subject. And so it has come about that, to-day, there is a steady and serious study of our subject going on around us. Not among one class of people or another, but by all sorts and conditions of men and women who are beginning to realise that what they have been taught about death and the after-life has been wrong.

All over the world Spiritualism is making its appeal as a reasonable and sensible belief.

One has only to read regularly the various Spiritualist journals to realise how increasingly the subject is being examined and investigated in almost every civilised country. We live in an age when people are thinking for themselves. No longer do they take everything for granted or believe everything they are told. Science is daily impressing them with the hitherto unrealised fact that the universe is only limited by the conception of it which man's mind is capable of assimilating. And as man's mind grows and widens, so the universe becomes to him a more wonderful and beautiful picture of reality.

Not only so, but as man's conception of his surroundings becomes clearer and deeper, so his conception of himself becomes similarly changed. He sees himself as part of a great cosmic whole, progressing and developing in accordance with the laws of Nature. No longer can he believe in any mythical " fall " in a mythical Garden of Eden through eating a mythical apple. Consequently, he realises the futility of a doctrine which sends a person to hell when he hasn't had a dog's chance on earth, or condemns him to everlasting punishment if he does not happen to be one of the favoured ones who were " predestinated " to eternal life before the world began.

Such doctrines are no longer preached from our pulpits. Why? Because every reasonable and intelligent person realises their absurdity, and only refers to them now as the antiquated beliefs of our ancestors. Orthodoxy is dead! It struggled hard for its very existence, but it was opposed by a relentless foe—common sense—and ultimately it was forced to succumb. Hints of its unlamented end have been thrown out from time to time by sundry of its friends, but its funeral was officially notified when Dean Inge, late of St. Paul's Cathedral, publicly announced that " no person could be orthodox unless he did not think."

That pronouncement, from the pen of such an eminent spokesman of the Church, was the reading of the burial service over the body of the departed, the committing of Orthodoxy to its grave, without even the customary " sure and certain hope " of a distant Resurrection morning. For people like to be thought intelligent; to tell a person that he does not think amounts almost to an insult. And the more people think the more do they desire to acquire knowledge. But their knowledge must fulfil one essential condition—it must appeal to reason.

Now Spiritualism, in spite of all the gibes and jeers which have been heaped upon it by narrow-minded and ignorant people in the past, is, I repeat, a reasonable and sensible belief. It may not appeal to the self-centred person whose outlook on life is bounded by his office desk on the one hand and his favourite night club on the other. It cannot appeal to the type of individual who has such a poor conception of himself that he believes he is only fit to snuff out like a candle at the end of life's short day and be no more. But it does appeal to the person who realises that there must be some purpose in life, and that, if that be the case, life must be worth living. And if life be worth living, it naturally follows that there must be something to be gained by living it well.

Here we find ourselves in the realm of the spiritual, not the material, aspect of existence, the realm which is embraced in the teachings of Spiritualism. There is no such word as "death" in the Spiritualist's vocabulary. Life continues. The grave does not wipe out the results of a mis-spent life, neither does it leave ungarnered the fruits of a life of self-sacrifice spent in the service of humanity. Spiritualism teaches that, just exactly as we live here, so shall we find ourselves when we have entered into the next stage of our existence— no better and no worse.

If we have done wrong here, we must right that wrong there before we can progress to a higher state of spiritual consciousness. On the other hand, if we have done well here, we shall find that spiritual part of us which survives the grave more purified, more refined, and more capable of enjoying those things " which God hath prepared for them that love Him."

That is why I say that Spiritualism is a reasonable and sensible belief. It conforms to the inexorable and unbreakable law of Cause and Effect. It appeals to the thinking man and woman of to-day. It is common sense.

And it has broken down the barrier between this stage of existence and the next, the barrier which has always been the one great problem and mystery of human life. When we lay the lifeless form in the grave we do not say " Good-bye." We know that our loved one is still with us—invisible, perhaps— but nevertheless just as real, just the same in every respect as when seen by our mortal eyes. And we know that, as opportunity offers, we can still speak with that loved one as of yore, that the emancipated spirit is not beyond our reach, but that " Earth is crammed with Heaven " and that death, so-called, is but the door into another room in our Father's house. And the door is *not* closed but always ajar, so that—

> . . . ever near us, though unseen,
> The dear immortal spirits tread ;
> For all the boundless universe
> Is life—there are no dead.

No wonder, then, that Spiritualism is gaining ground. It teaches Knowledge, not blind credulity ; Facts, not thoughtless faith. That is why it appeals, and must inevitably continue to appeal, to thinking people throughout the world.

CHAPTER II.

IS INQUIRY JUSTIFIED?

A FRIEND, with whom I was discussing Spiritualism recently, summed up his opinion on the subject in these words—" Well," he said, " I am not too sure about it. I can't help thinking that we are not meant to inquire into the hereafter."

There are many people who view the matter in that light. They have an uncanny feeling that there must be something wrong in investigating a subject which they have been brought up to regard with a mixture of awe and fear. To them, death and the hereafter, as a topic of inquiry or even of conversation, should be avoided.

But why? If a person admits fear of death, that can only be for one of two reasons. Either he has an uneasy conscience or else he has an entirely wrong conception of what death really is. And in both of these cases the sooner he rectifies his error, and finds out what lies before him, the better. The only person who logically should have no interest in the subject is the Materialist—the man who has convinced himself that human existence begins with the cradle and ends with the grave. To him, death is the end of all things so far as he, personally, is concerned, and as there is

consequently no hereafter there is no subject
for inquiry. The orthodox believer, too, might
claim exemption from investigating the matter
on the grounds that he has already been
" predestinated " to a future life of bliss or woe,
and that as his ultimate fate is thus decided in
advance no amount of inquiry can possibly change it.

But the great majority of people are neither
Materialists nor Fundamentalists. They are
ordinary every-day folk who take an intelligent
interest in life and instinctively hold the conviction
that somewhere, and in some form, they will
continue to exist when that life, so far as this
world is concerned, is over. Why, then, should
they not inquire into what that future state holds
for them ? If knowledge on the subject is available,
surely it is not only natural, but advisable, to try
and discover all there is to be known about it.
A person planning to emigrate, say, to Australia,
where he intends to settle down and spend the
rest of his life, would indeed be foolish if he failed
to acquire as much information about the country
of his future domicile as was humanly possible.
Few of us may desire to emigrate and are therefore
not called upon to make such plans. But all of us,
whether we desire it or not, must make the final
journey which we call " death," and that journey,
if an after-life exists at all, must bring us to some
new country where our future life is to be spent.

Is there any sound justification, then, for the
argument that we are not " meant " to know what
must of necessity lie before each one of us ?
If there is, the Churches have been greatly at fault

in expressing so forcibly their ideas on the subject.
It is no more harmful to *know* than to *believe*.
"Seek after knowledge," said Solomon. "Add
to your faith, knowledge," said Peter. So, at least,
Spiritualists can claim that in furthering their
inquiries into the hereafter they are only obeying
these two Biblical injunctions.

But that is just where we fall foul of our critics.
They reply, "No, you are not supposed to know
anything about the hereafter ; you must walk by
faith." That may be all very well, but walking
by faith is like any other walk you may take.
If you do not know the road you are walking you
are apt to get lost. And before you can walk by
faith you must at least know what particular
faith you are going to walk by.

On a certain Sunday evening in London, a few
years ago, a Bishop of the Church of England,
Dr. Winnington Ingram, preached a sermon on the
subject of "Death and the Hereafter." He told
his congregation that, when a person died, he was
as much alive again, in heaven, five minutes after
death as he had been alive on earth five minutes
before it. In another church, not far away, another
sermon was being preached, in this case, against
Spiritualism, by a well-known Doctor of Divinity,
Dr. J. Stuart Holden. This preacher informed his
hearers that, when a person died, he remained in a
state of sleep until the glorious coming of the
Lord on the Resurrection morning.

Now, even at the risk of appearing frivolous,
let us imagine that some friend who had lost a
loved one, and was anxious to obtain information

on this vitally important question, was in London on that particular Sunday, and had been able to listen to both of these sermons.   He certainly could not doubt the authority of the preachers.   Both had gone through a lengthy course of University training.   Both had made a careful study of Theology.   Both accepted the Bible as the Word of God.   Both were recognised experts on their subject.   But, in spite of all that, I cannot help thinking that our friend would be puzzled.   One of these learned gentlemen had told him one thing, the other had told him the exact opposite.

I hardly imagine that he would be satisfied.

So, as he walks along the street, trying to make sense of it all, he sees another church and decides to make further inquiries there.   He is met by a kindly priest who assures him that he can answer his question.   Both of the other preachers are wrong, he tells him.   What actually happens after death is that a person goes to a place called Purgatory and there he remains for an indefinite period of time.   No, it is not a nice place, rather the reverse ; so much so that anyone who has a loved one there should do everything in his power to secure his release as soon as possible.   How can that be done ?   Oh, quite easily.   If our friend will give him, the priest, a pound note he will undertake to say a number of masses for the soul of the departed, and in some mysterious way that will " do the trick."   Of course, if a pound's worth of masses is found to be insufficient, no doubt our friend would not grudge another pound later on.

But our friend is not convinced. He would like a little time to think it over.

Again he finds himself in the street, and after further thought he comes to the conclusion that perhaps, after all, this priest was right. Where is this "heaven" the Bishop spoke of? He didn't seem to know. And when is this "Resurrection morning" to which the Doctor of Divinity so glibly referred? They were both very hazy about the whole subject, whereas the priest had at least appealed to his business instincts. Anyway, it was worth trying. So he stops at the next church he comes to, on the notice-board outside of which he reads the words "Methodist Chapel." He doesn't exactly know what the term means, but he boldly goes inside and offers the minister a pound note in payment for the usual number of masses being said to rescue a soul from purgatory!

I need not carry this imaginary incident any further. Instead of speaking with one united voice, our religious teachers all have their own ideas on the subject of life after death. No wonder the man in the street is puzzled and confused.

But although our spiritual advisers differ in their opinions concerning the hereafter, there is one subject on which, officially at least, they maintain complete unanimity. That is Spiritualism. Bishops, Doctors of Divinity, Roman Catholic priests and Methodist pastors all condemn it. I say "officially," because, as I have already stated, many of them know, and some openly admit, the truth of its claims and teaching. But the Christian Church, as a body, rejects it. It points an

admonitory finger to certain obscure verses in the
Old Testament which refer to familiar spirits,
necromancy, and so on, and solemnly pronounces
its verdict that all such allusions refer to Spiritualism,
and prove that God has forbidden any intercourse
between us and those beyond the veil of death.
If they are right, only one conclusion can be drawn.
God has mightily changed since the days of Moses.
The whole record of the Bible, from Genesis to
Revelation, is full of instances of spirit intercourse. From beginning to end the Bible is a
Spiritualist text book, and I do not hesitate to
add that only a Spiritualist can fully understand it.

After about twenty years of concentrated study
on the part of sixty-four leading theological students
of eminence a volume was produced entitled
" A New Commentary on Holy Scripture." When
they reached the 12th chapter of 1st Corinthians,
which begins " Now concerning spiritual gifts,
brethren, I would not have you ignorant," they
found themselves hopelessly out of their depth.
Among these gifts, Paul tells us, is the gift of
" discerning of spirits." Surely a simple and
straightforward sentence, consisting of three
commonly used English words, which hardly
requires to be commented on at all ! But here
is how its meaning was elucidated by these sixty-four
theologians—

> " That discerning of spirits appears as a
> spiritual gift shows that it was not always
> easy to be certain of the value and authority
> of a spiritual utterance."

But surely the words " discerning of spirits "
mean just exactly what they say—no more and
no less. If you are a golfer and your ball is lying
nicely on the green, why throw it into a bunker?
The words mean " discerning of spirits," and for
the life of me I cannot see how anybody can possibly
make them mean anything else. Every leading
character in the Bible, from Adam in the Garden
of Eden to John on the Island of Patmos, discerned
spirits. It was such a regular, everyday occurrence
in those times that the fact is consistently recorded
without any special comment. And yet the
authors of " The New Commentary " appear to
be blissfully unaware of the elementary meaning
of these three simple words!

It is unfortunately true that many people fight
shy of making any inquiry into Spiritualism
because they are afraid of what their friends might
say if they knew they were interested in the subject.
These people lack the courage of their convictions.
I do not say that all of them would deny the truth
of Spiritualism if the occasion arose, but they
prefer to keep silence rather than confess their
knowledge in the presence of others. On the
other hand I know a number of men who take no
outward interest in the subject, and who refrain
from attending Spiritualist meetings, because they
know that to do so would prejudice them in the
eyes of their business associates. The fault is not
altogether theirs. They have their means of
livelihood to consider, and to that extent they are
not free agents. The pity is that, in this 20th
century and in a country which makes such a

profession of religious freedom and equality, a state of affairs should exist which permits this kind of persecution to take place.

But others are not so blameless. As I write, I am thinking of a certain prominent man in a fair-sized town. He is well-known and respected by all. He has spent many years of his life in local administrative and philanthropic work, which has brought him before a public who seek his advice and admire his character. For years that man has been interested in Spiritualism. He has asked me to lend him books on the subject ; he attends Spiritualist meetings when he is away from home, where he is unknown. Not long ago a Spiritualist Association was formed in his home town, and a church was opened which holds services every Sunday evening. Shortly after this I met the man and said to him, " I hear you have a Spiritualist Association in your town now ; you'll be joining it, I suppose." Oh, no ! " was his reply, " I'm too well known there to be identified with anything like that ! "

That man was a moral coward. In fact, he was worse than that. He knew the value of Spiritualism ; he had had experience of the comfort it brings to those in sorrow. And yet he deliberately withheld his knowledge and influence in case this might adversely affect his popularity. It is people such as these who will suffer when they have passed on to the Other Side of Life. The moralists can say what they like, but sins of commission are by no means the only ones we shall have to reckon with when that time comes. Sins of *omission* are of no less vital importance, and many a departed spirit has come back and confessed that bigotry and lack of moral courage has been the transgression which has hindered his progress in the after-life.

In that remarkable book, "The Scripts of Cleophas," written by automatic writing through the hand of Miss Geraldine Cummins, we read how, when Paul returned to Jerusalem after one of his early missionary journeys, he learned that his father was also in the city. His father sends for him and tries to persuade him to give up this "new sect" to which he has attached himself. At first he speaks to him in a friendly way, but when he finds that Paul remains firm in his resolve he loses his temper and blazes out upon him with these words—"If thou wilt not give up this new sect," he exclaims, "I shall cast thee from me; tear thee from my heart as the great wind teareth the roots of a tree from the ground. Thou shalt have no part or lot in my possessions. . . . From henceforth, if thou heedest me not, thou shalt labour with thy hands, for my curse shall go with thee."

So Paul was cast out of his father's house. And the first person he meets is his friend, Timothy, to whom he says—"Timothy, I have given up all for Christ. Go thou, and do likewise, and together we shall go again and preach the gospel to the Gentiles."

When I first read these words I was struck by the noble simplicity of this man. We may not agree with Paul's theology, but at least we can be broadminded enough to admire his courage.

He was prepared to " give up all " for what he believed to be true.

Luigi Galvani, the 18th century Italian scientist, was considered by all his friends to be mad. They laughed and jeered at him, and at first sight there appears to have been good reason for their doing so. Because his chief hobby seemed to be putting live frogs into a glass bowl filled with water, and then passing an electric current through the water and watching the frogs' legs twitch as a result of the charge affecting their muscles. But his only reply to all the scoffers was " never mind, posterity will yet bless me." And posterity has blessed him, many times over, because as a result of his experiments there came to be invented what is known as the Galvanic battery, out of which has grown the great science of electrical treatment for muscular diseases of all sorts, which treatment is now obtainable in all our hospitals and nursing homes. Galvani did not bother about the scoffing and the criticism. He knew what he was doing, and was so convinced that he was right that he was quite prepared to be thought mad, and to give up his popularity, knowing that posterity would bless him in the end.

Each of these men, in his own sphere, displayed a moral courage which many people lack to-day. They ignored opposition and steadfastly pursued the path which they believed to be right. Compare their conduct with that of the man who refused to identify himself with Spiritualism because doing so might adversely affect his popularity. What is your verdict ? Which of the three do you admire,

which do you despise? Every person who has
had the claims of Spiritualism brought to his
notice is in the same position as each of these men.
He must either be afraid to investigate the subject
and acknowledge defeat, or he must have the courage
of his convictions and ignore all opposition. There
is no middle road.

There is only one question which the prospective
inquirer needs to ask himself. Is this inquiry
likely to do me any good? If he conscientiously
feels that it will not, then let him drop the subject
at once. He will only be wasting his time. On the
other hand, if he feels that seeking after, and
obtaining, this knowledge of the hereafter will
do him good, then obviously there can be nothing
wrong in proceeding with his investigation. The
testimony of many famous men and women answers
that question in the affirmative, without
qualification or reserve. William Ewart Gladstone,
when he was Prime Minister, stated " Psychical
Research is the most important work which is
being done in the world—by far the most important."
Would such a man, in his position, make so emphatic
a statement if he did not honestly believe that this
work was doing good? And did it not do good
to John Ruskin who, after abandoning his
Materialistic beliefs, boldly declared " What has
caused the change in my views is the unanswerable
evidence of Spiritualism."

The following story was told me by Lady
Conan Doyle.

Two friends of Sir Arthur were walking along
Oxford Street in London one night when they

saw a little way ahead of them a young man who was evidently the worse of drink. The names of the two friends were the Rev. Mr. Crewe, an American clergyman, and Mr. Phillips. The former, Mr. Crewe, was clairvoyant. Mr. Phillips said to him, " Just look at that young man ; isn't that a sad sight? " " Yes," replied Mr. Crewe, " but if you could see what I see you would say it was sadder still. Because I see clairvoyantly the figure of a woman walking by that man's side. I think it must be his mother and she seems to be pleading with him." The two friends quickened their pace and overtook the young man. They spoke to him and Mr. Crewe described the figure whom he had seen beside him. " I think she was your mother," he said. They obtained the man's address and the next day they called on him. While Mr. Phillips was speaking to him Mr. Crewe suddenly felt impelled to go into trance. The man's mother took control of him. She began by repeating the last words she had spoken to him on earth. Then she sang a hymn which she had been in the habit of singing to him as a child, after which she spoke to him. She talked as only a mother can talk to her son who has gone wrong. When Mr. Crewe came out of trance he found the young man sobbing with his face in his hands, in a state of deep distress.

Shortly afterwards Sir Arthur Conan Doyle received a long letter from this man. It ended with the words, " This is my tribute to your cause. I swear I shall never go wrong again." Sir Arthur sent the letter to an uncle of the man, who was one of the highest dignitaries of the Church of England.

He wrote him a personal letter in which he said,
" I will not mention your name, but here is your
sister's son saved by your sister whom you call
" dead." Never again say that this thing is of
the devil ; it is of the angels."

Did Spiritualism do that young man any good ?
Let our critics think carefully before they answer.

But there is another side to the picture. That
man was not inquiring into the hereafter. In
fact, I imagine that the hereafter was probably
the last thing he ever thought about. It was his
mother, in the " hereafter," who was inquiring
about him.

Some people tell us that we should not
" disturb the dead." They do not seem to realise
that it is the " dead " who sometimes disturb us.
Whether we inquire into the hereafter, or not ;
whether we think it right to do so, or wrong ;
the fact still remains that the Spirit World is there,
and our friends who are in the Spirit World are not
always so willing to ignore us as we, in our stupidity,
are sometimes willing to ignore them. To be
content with ignorance, and refuse to make this
inquiry, may seem an easy road for the indolent
and timid, who shrink from anything that might
unsettle their pre-conceived ideas. But that is a
selfish attitude to adopt. It never seems to occur
to these people that, if Spiritualism be true, their
loved ones on the Other Side may be wanting to
get in touch with them.

How different is the mental attitude of such
people compared with that of the Spiritualist
who can truthfully say that he has obeyed the

injunction, " Seek and ye shall find ! " Because
they who seek, do find—they find a peace and
happiness in life which nothing can destroy. They
find that fears caused by ignorance have vanished,
that the gloom of vague hopes and beliefs has
given place to the sunshine of knowledge, and
that henceforth they and their unseen friends
will go forward in an unbroken companionship
which not even death can sever.

CHAPTER III.

EARLY DAYS.

I HAVE already said that Spiritualism, by whatever name it may have been known in the past, is as old as the human race. To trace its history in any detail would require not one but many volumes, and it is no part of my task to attempt to do so, even in brief. What is termed Modern Spiritualism came into existence in 1848, but prior to that date two outstanding incidents took place in this country which are worthy of mention.

The first of these was the strange event which happened in the vicarage of Epworth in 1715. In that vicarage was born the founder of Methodism, John Wesley, and in the year I have mentioned peculiar rappings were heard throughout the house which disturbed and alarmed its occupants. As these continued, however, the family began to treat the matter as a joke. Nevertheless, they appear to have realised that the sounds were caused by some discarnate form of intelligence, as they gave " it " a name. " Old Jeffrey," they called it. Had the incident been taken more seriously, and the implications which lay behind the rappings been considered and understood, there is no saying what far-reaching consequences might have ensued.

Unfortunately, however, Wesley was convinced that the phenomenon could only bode harm to those in the house, so he called in a number of other clergymen, and they all prayed fervently that God would cause the spirit to take its departure. Needless to say, the spirit, without waiting for any further request, did so. And so the matter ended.

The other incident, or series of incidents, occurred about the year 1830, in Regent Square Church, London, of which the pastor at that time was a man named Edward Irving. Irving was born at Annan, in Dumfriesshire, in 1792. He had been brought up in the narrow-minded atmosphere of an 18th century Presbyterian household and eventually entered the Church, becoming assistant to the famous Dr. Chalmers, one of the most renowned clergymen that the Presbyterian Church in Scotland has ever produced.

Irving was a great preacher. His sermons drew large congregations, and before long he moved to London and became the minister of Regent Square Church. All went well until strange manifestations began to take place during the services. The " gift of tongues " suddenly descended upon certain members of the congregation, who would rise to their feet and commence, so we are told, to hold forth in unknown languages. Probably, however, this is an exaggeration. What is more likely is that the controlling spirit, or spirits, were merely attempting to obtain control of their vocal organs, and in this they eventually appear to have succeeded. Before long, words and sentences which gradually became more intelligible came to be spoken, and as time went on long speeches were made by one or other of those " possessed." During these, a wide field of topics was covered, but they mainly dealt with sundry abstruse points of doctrine. To what extent these occurrences were due to psychic influence, it is hard to say. Certain it is that matters soon drifted into a state of chaos, owing to a complete ignorance of the laws governing spiritual manifestations on the part of those concerned, preventing any semblance of order and coherence being maintained.

Eventually Irving was deposed from his ministry by the General Assembly of the Church of Scotland, and became one of the founders of the Catholic Apostolic Church. There seems no doubt that, however much these strange outbursts were due to hysteria or undue excitement on the part of the participants, a certain amount of genuine psychic power lay behind them.

I have referred to them, and to the earlier rappings in the vicarage of Epworth, because it is not beyond the bounds of probability that both point in the same direction. In both cases men of strong and outstanding personality were concerned. Both of these men were clergymen. We are told, and there is good reason to accept it as true, that there is a deliberate and organised effort being made in the Spirit World to bring the truth of survival, and of the possibility of communication between the two worlds, to the dwellers on this earth. And to whom would it be most likely that this truth should first be brought ? Surely to the Church, the custodian of our religious teaching, whose duty it is to prepare us for death and the hereafter.

The Church has always taught that an after-life exists. What, then, would be more natural than that those who were engaged in this task in the Unseen should endeavour, first of all, to impress the Church with the importance of their mission and the truth of the message they sought to convey? They were merely bringing proof of what the Church already believed and preached. Had more intelligence and less prejudice been exhibited in both of these cases, it is difficult to assess what might have been the ultimate value to humanity of these demonstrations of psychic power. But the Church refused to countenance them. In both cases their origin was attributed to the devil. The prayers at Epworth, and the hisses and hoots of disapproval which greeted the manifestations at Regent Square, must have convinced the unseen would-be benefactors of the human race that a Church, creed-bound and ignorant of the nature of psychic gifts, was not the medium through which new truths could be conveyed.

" Thou hast hid these things from the wise and prudent, and hast revealed them unto babes." These words appear to be as true to-day as when they were uttered nineteen hundred years ago. So the workers in the Unseen desisted from their attempts to convince those who should have been most easily convinced, and turned their attention elsewhere.

And it was to " babes " they went.

In the year 1848 there lived in a small village called Hydesville, in the State of New York, a humble family named Fox. Besides the father and mother there were two children at home, both girls—Margaret, aged fourteen, and Kate, aged eleven. In this lowly dwelling rappings began to be heard, similar to those which had disturbed the peace of mind of the Vicar of Epworth nearly a century and a half before. But in this case the occupants of the house approached the problem with a lesser degree of religious superstition and a greater degree of intelligence. They set themselves the task of trying to ascertain the cause of the disturbance.

John D. Fox and his wife were two of the earliest of modern psychic researchers ! When one of them hid behind one side of the door on which the rappings were taking place, and the other hid behind the other, in an endeavour to trace their cause, they were unconsciously helping to lay the foundation stone of that great edifice of psychic knowledge, the building of which is far from being completed even to-day, although work upon it has been in progress for nigh on one hundred years. And their simple searching did not go unrewarded, although the credit for the success achieved must mainly go to the "babes" of the family, Margaret and Kate.

On the night of 31st March, 1848, the rappings were louder than usual, so much so that the entire family were roused from their beds. Then a trifling incident occurred—trifling in itself, but destined to be of world-wide importance. One of the girls snapped her fingers. On such seemingly insignificant actions do the destinies of humanity sometimes depend ! The snap of the fingers was answered by a rap. The experiment, if such it can be called, was repeated. So was the rap. Communication with the Unseen had been established in an intelligent form. Then the mother asked a question. How many children had she? Seven raps were given in reply. Mrs. Fox at once exclaimed that this number was wrong. The seven raps were repeated. Then she remembered that, while six of her children were still living, one had died in early life.

Soon a rude form of alphabet was devised, and in this way answers were received to further questions. It was not long before neighbours came to join in these strange proceedings, and when at length somebody thought of asking the " rapper " if he could give his name, he did so without delay. Charles B. Rosma, he spelt out. He went on to state that he had been murdered in that house a few years previously and that his body was buried in the cellar. There the body was ultimately discovered, and Rosma was found to have been a pedlar who had last been seen in that locality but had mysteriously disappeared.

Margaret and Kate Fox were mediums ; two of these gifted persons in whose presence, even in childhood, psychic phenomena can be produced. Both became famous in that capacity in later years, as did also a third sister, Leah, who was not living at home when this incident occurred.

The happenings at Hydesville became widely known throughout the United States and aroused tremendous interest, coupled with a veritable tornado of abuse directed against the Fox family by the champions of narrow-minded sectarianism. The two girls were forced to leave home, as life there became intolerable for them, Kate going to stay with her brother and Margaret taking refuge with her sister, Leah. In both of these houses the raps immediately began, especially in the latter, where they were exceptionally violent, doubtless because of the extra psychic power drawn from two mediums instead of from one.

The subsequent career of the Fox sisters is now a matter of history. The story has frequently been recounted, and will be found at considerable length in Sir Arthur Conan Doyle's "History of Spiritualism." How the girls lived through these early years it is hard to understand. They were completely at the mercy of numerous so-called "investigators," whose object in parading them before a curious and incredulous public appears to have been chiefly that of financial gain. Nobody understood, in these early days, the extremely delicate nature of what was taking place, or the danger to which the girls' health was being exposed through long and frequent sittings, often with people who bullied and harried them if the phenomena did not come up to their expectations.

On more than one occasion their lives were definitely in danger. But through it all they had at least one staunch advocate and supporter, Mr. Horace Greeley, editor of the " New York

Tribune " and afterwards a candidate for the Presidency of the United States. Spiritualists owe this man a debt of gratitude, not only for his unswerving belief in the genuineness of the phenomena, but also, and perhaps even to a greater extent, for his constant friendly interest in the girls themselves during the early days of their mediumistic career.

Another notable man who was convinced by these rappings was John Worth Edmonds, former Senator and afterwards Judge of the Supreme Court of New York State. He investigated the matter carefully, and his conclusions were confirmed when later his own daughter developed mediumship, speaking in foreign languages of which she had no knowledge, and clairvoyantly describing spirit forms who were recognised by people whom she had never previously met.

Between 1850 and 1855 Judge Edmonds published his experiences in two volumes, which were widely read, the Hydesville episode and the widespread interest it had aroused having caused a tremendous demand for literature on the subject.

In these early days the phenomena were crude in the extreme. With the exception of a few outstanding figures, such as Andrew Jackson Davis and Daniel Dunglas Home, most of the early mediums were only able to produce communications in the form of raps, table tilting and telekinesis— the movement of objects without any physical contact. Mental phenomena, such as trance speaking, clairvoyance and clairaudience, were comparatively rare. The explanation of this appears to lie in the desire of those in the Spirit World to attract attention to their activities, and to ensure that these received the widest publicity. Human nature being what it is, an oration spoken by a person in trance, no matter how eloquently it may be declaimed, interests a much smaller circle of people than, say, a flower vase being hurled through a window without any visible form of force behind it.

It is hardly a matter of surprise that timid and superstitious people put that sort of performance down to the machinations of the devil and his satelites. The subject had never been scientifically and rationally examined. At the best any explanations which could be given were no more than theories based on inadequate experience. But even so, I imagine there were few who went so far as a certain stalwart son of Protestantism, a clergyman in the West of England, who stoutly and volubly maintained that the communicating intelligences were evilly disposed spirits whose headquarters were in Rome, and who were incited to their sinful occupation by the head of their nefarious organisation, who also lived in that historic and ancient city !

For some years interest in Spiritualism centred chiefly in the United States, but gradually it gathered strength in this country. This was greatly due to the arrival from America of a remarkable medium, Mrs. Hayden, who, during a year's sojourn in England, held many seances and planted the seeds of Spiritualism which were destined to take root and flourish in the years which followed.

Then came Daniel Dunglas Home, one of the greatest mediums of last century.

D. D. Home, as he is usually called, was born near Edinburgh in 1833. His mother came from the Highlands and was gifted with what is there known as "second sight." So there is not much doubt from which side of the family he derived his mediumistic tendencies. When about nine years of age he went with an aunt to America, and it was there that he first showed signs of his psychic powers. When he was thirteen years old he had a school friend named Edwin, and one day, after the two boys had been reading a ghost story, they made a compact that, if one of them should die, he would come back and tell the other. Shortly after this, Edwin's parents moved to another part of the country, so the boys lost touch with one another. Home had no reason to think that his friend was ill, but one night, just after he had got into bed, Edwin suddenly appeared beside him and said that he had come to keep his promise. Home told his aunt of this occurrence, and two or three days later the news was confirmed by a letter from Edwin's parents saying that he had died on the same day as he had appeared to Home.

About four years after this episode, Home had another similar experience. This time his mother appeared to him, telling him that she had died that day at precisely 12 o'clock. This, too, was subsequently proved to be true. Other incidents followed. Rappings began to be heard in the house and small articles of furniture were moved in a seemingly mysterious way. But Home's aunt was of the rigid, orthodox type ; this sort of thing was too much for her. So she called in, first, a Wesleyan minister, then a Congregationalist minister, and, finally, a Baptist minister, in order, as she said, " to drive the devil out of the boy." In turn they prayed and read the Bible, they scolded and threatened, but when none of these methods proved to be of any avail, the aunt took the law into her own hands. She turned the boy out of doors, saying that she would not have the devil living any longer under her roof. Such was the tragic result, in Home's case, of bigoted and superstitious ignorance.

Unfortunately, Home was a delicate lad. He studied medicine with the intention of becoming a doctor, but his health gave way and he was advised to take a sea voyage. Accordingly, he decided to pay a visit to this country. He had a small private income, and all his life he made this do for his modest requirements. Never in all his long mediumistic career, extending over thirty years, did he accept a penny for all the thousands of seances and sittings he gave, not only in this country and America, but in the many countries he visited on the continent of Europe. On one occasion he was offered a fee of £2,000 if he would give a seance for a number of wealthy men in Paris. He gave seance, but he refused the money. So it cannot be said, in Home's case, that profit was an incentive to fraud, a charge which is so maliciously and untruthfully brought against mediums, even to-day.

When he arrived in this country, at the age of twenty-two, he travelled to London and took rooms at Cox's Hotel in Jermyn Street, the proprietor of which, as it happened, was already interested in Spiritualism. Consequently, it was not long before his name became well known. He gave hundreds of sittings to various members of different Societies —scientific, literary and medical—as well as to many groups of private individuals ; but although some people condemned him, as was only to be expected, during his whole career he was never convicted of any semblance of fraud. After sitting with him on over fifty different occasions and knowing him for many years, the famous scientist, Sir William Crookes, wrote, " I never once had the slightest suspicion that he was attempting to play any tricks. He was scrupulously honest. To those who knew him, Home was one of the most lovable of men, and his perfect genuineness and uprightness were beyond suspicion."

One of Home's strongest powers was that of levitation, that is, being lifted by unseen forces, sometimes as high as the ceiling. Numerous instances of this might be given, the best known being one which took place at a sitting given by him in Ashley House, London. A number of prominent men were present, when suddenly Home was lifted out of his chair, turned horizontally in the air, and lying at full length in this position he slowly drifted out of the open window, seventy feet above the street. Those present watched this amazing phenomenon, expecting every moment to see him crash to the ground. But Home turned—or rather, I should say, *was* turned by some unseen force— in mid-air and drifted back into the house again through another open window in an adjoining room.

He repeated this twice at the same sitting. Those who had witnessed this amazing incident all signed a statement, testifying that they had seen it occur. On this occasion Home was in trance, but frequently he was levitated while in a state of normal consciousness. At times he would take a pencil from his pocket and make a mark, or sign his name, on the ceiling, so as to convince the sitters that they were not the victims of their imagination.

Owing to his delicate state of health Home had to spend part of each year abroad. His fame soon followed him there. In this country he had given sittings to various members of the Royal Family; in Paris he was summoned to the presence of the Emperor, Napoleon III. Both the Emperor and the Empress were intensely interested in Home's psychic powers, so much so that the Church authorities in France went out of their way to contradict a rumour that the Emperor was interested in Spiritualism! On various occasions the Church, both at home and abroad, went to almost unbelievable lengths to try and bring Home into disrepute. In Italy, for example, it denounced him as a sorceror and forced the police to expel him from Rome. On his return home he laid a formal complaint before the Foreign Office. The subject was even raised in Parliament, but nothing came of this, as the matter was quietly hushed up.

Home's fame spread all over the continent. There was hardly a Royal Palace in Europe where he was not known and received on terms of friendship. He was of a shy and retiring disposition, passionately fond of painting, sculpture and music.

He was a deeply religious man, and when even kings and queens asked him if he could explain his extraordinary powers, his answer was always the same, " God has given me these gifts. I cannot explain them. I can only carry out my mission."

Another of Home's gifts was the ability to handle fire without being burned. When told by his spirit guides that he could safely do so, he would take a red hot coal from the fire, hold it in his hand and walk about the room. Once he held a burning coal between both of his hands and blew on them like a bellows, until the flames licked up through his fingers. One of those present exclaimed, " Isn't it wonderful ? " to which Home replied simply, " God is wonderful ; so are His laws." Never, in spite of hardship or persecution, did he lose this simple faith in God's goodness. He attributed all his amazing powers to Him. And yet, as Sir Arthur Conan Doyle remarked, " As for the clergy, they might not have existed during the thirty years that this, the most marvellous spiritual outpouring of many centuries, was before the public. One cannot recall the name of one British clergyman who showed any intelligent interest in the subject ; and when in 1872 a full account of the St. Petersburg seances began to appear in " The Times," it was cut short on account of strong remonstrances to the editor by certain of the clergy of the Church of England. Such was the contribution of our official spiritual guides."

Home died in France in 1886, and the epitaph on his tombstone is taken from the verse in

Corinthians, " To another is given the discerning of spirits." Near the Parish Church in the Canongate, in Edinburgh, a fountain has been erected to his memory.

Perhaps I cannot close this very brief sketch of his career more fittingly than by quoting some of his own words, taken from a lecture which he gave in London while still at the height of his power. " I believe," he said, " in my heart that this power is being spread more and more every day to draw us nearer to God. It teaches us that He is Love and that there is no death. To the aged it comes as a solace, when the storms of life are nearly over ; to the young it speaks of the duty we owe each other, and that as we sow so shall we reap. It comes to roll away the clouds of error and to bring nearer the bright morning of a never-ending day."

Another of the great pioneers to whom Spiritualists owe much was Mrs. Emma Hardinge Britten, who was not only a great medium but also the author of many books on psychic and religious subjects.

Mrs. Britten was the daughter of a sea captain and was an accomplished musician. She became interested in Spiritualism in 1856 and shortly afterwards developed strong psychic powers. Her name attained considerable publicity through a remarkable piece of evidence for survival which she gave when the steamship " Pacific " was lost in an Atlantic gale. One of the crew, who had been drowned, controlled Mrs. Britten and recounted the story of what had taken place.

This information was, of course, unknown to any person on shore. The owners of the vessel threatened to prosecute her, on the grounds that she had caused unnecessary alarm, but before proceedings could be taken the information given through her mediumship was proved to be true.

Her mediumistic gifts covered a much wider range than those generally in evidence at that time. When in trance she was an eloquent speaker, discoursing on a variety of subjects which were far beyond her normal knowledge. Over a period of years she travelled extensively in many parts of the world, proclaiming and demonstrating the claims of Spiritualism, but she is probably remembered best among present-day Spiritualists as the medium through whom were given the Seven Principles of Spiritualism, and as the founder and editor, for five years, of the weekly paper, " The Two Worlds."

Mr. James Robertson, author of " Spiritualism ; the Open Door to the Unseen Universe," who knew Mrs. Britten intimately, writes of her as follows :—" She was certainly one of the most brilliant women I have ever met. A storehouse of rich knowledge came to her from her friends in the unseen. She gave us some graphic pictures of a visit to Monte Carlo, which showed how real was obsession, even in our day, and which made the stories in the New Testament of such occurrences look like actual facts. With her clairvoyant vision she had seen the ghosts of those who had gone out of life standing by the victims of gambling, luring them on. So dramatic was her speech that

one could almost see the scene as it occurred . . .
She knew Abraham Lincoln intimately, and had
in her possession a portrait which his widow had
obtained when she went unknown and disguised
to a spirit photographer, a real portrait of the
murdered President, differing from any that had
ever been taken. Her own experiences of this
phase of spirit phenomena had been most varied.
She told the story of how, in the early days of her
mediumship, Beethoven had come to her, and as
she doubted his identity he told her he would give
her three tests. One came to pass the next day
about a musical criticism she was writing; another
when one of Beethoven's symphonies was played
by spirit hands; and a third when, with a friend,
she went to a photographer in Boston and there
appeared upon the plate, beside her, the form of
Beethoven, with a lyre formed of flowers."

In the space at my disposal it is impossible to
mention, even briefly, the great work done by
many of the leading figures of Spiritualism in the
latter half of last century. But no account, however
short, would be complete without some reference
to the mediumship of the Rev. Stainton Moses.

Born in 1839, Stainton Moses entered the
Church of England after completing his education
at Exeter College, Oxford. In 1872 he became
interested in Spiritualism, and before long he
discovered that he, himself, possessed the gift of
mediumship. This covered a wide field of
phenomena. Heavy tables would suddenly begin
to rock backwards and forwards in broad daylight
when nobody was near them. Objects from

different parts of the house were brought into the room in which he was sitting, through closed and locked doors. At times the room would suddenly be filled with a sweet perfume. Strains of music were frequently heard by all present, even although no musical instrument was in the house. But the greatest work he achieved lay in the field of automatic writing, through which he gave to the world a number of books, including "Spirit Teachings," which has frequently been described as "The Spiritualists' Bible."

As a clergyman, Stainton Moses belonged to the evangelical school of thought, and for a time he was deeply concerned at the trend of this new teaching, which was contrary to his own cherished beliefs. Frequently, after reading over what he had written, he would be so shocked at the statements made that he would express his strong disapproval or ask the communicators to elucidate some points with which he disagreed. This was always done at the next sitting. Eventually the communicators disclosed that they were the mouthpiece of a definite effort which was being made in the Spirit World to raise the human race to a higher level of thought, and that he had been chosen as their instrument on earth for this purpose.

But he was well aware of the possibility that his own mind might be unconsciously playing some part in the contents of these scripts. In this connection he wrote :—

"It is an interesting subject for speculation whether my own thoughts entered into the

4

subject matter of the communications. I took extraordinary pains to prevent any such admixture. At first the writing was slow, and it was necessary for me to follow it with my eye, but even then the thoughts were not my thoughts. Very soon the messages assumed a character of which I had no doubt whatever that the thought was opposed to my own. But I cultivated the power of occupying my mind with other things during the time that the writing was going on, and was able to read an abstruse book and follow out a line of close reasoning while the message was written with unbroken regularity. Messages so written extended over many pages, and in their course there was no correction, no fault in composition and often a sustained vigour and beauty of style."

The great work which Stainton Moses did for Spiritualism can hardly be over-estimated. Apart from his writings, which still enjoy wide publicity, he took an active part in its affairs, being for many years president of the London Spiritualist Alliance and editor of "Light." It is no exaggeration to say that his contribution to Spiritualism, coming when it did, raised the whole subject to a higher level than that in which he found it. In the words of F. W. H. Myers, his was "one of the most noteworthy lives of our generation." Greatly through his influence a new era of Spiritualism began, in which its philosophy became more widely studied and understood.

CHAPTER IV.

MY INTRODUCTION TO SPIRITUALISM.

IT was in 1919 that I first began to take an interest in Spiritualism. Shortly after the Armistice in November, 1918, I met with an accident which kept me on crutches for several weeks. As the doctor could not give a definite date when I would again be fit for duty, I was notified that my papers had been sent in to the War Office and that I would be free to return to civilian life as soon as my name appeared in the "Gazette." I was thus demobilised early in 1919, and went to stay for a few days with my brother whom I had not seen for some months.

He told me that he had had a strange experience at a Spiritualist seance, but such was my ignorance of the subject that I had to ask him a number of elementary questions as to what the term exactly meant. When he said that he believed he had been speaking to our father, who had died twelve years previously, I am afraid I was more amused than convinced. At the same time the serious way in which my brother spoke certainly impressed me, and when he produced a number of books on the subject, written by men whose names are household words, I realised that we were dealing with a subject which was of much greater importance than I had imagined.

My brother lent me one or two of these books which I read with growing interest.

But other matters claimed my more immediate attention. I had to return to the office and pick up the threads of business once again. So I had little leisure to devote to study of any kind beyond business affairs. Then one morning my brother came into my room in the office and asked me if I would care to go with him that afternoon to a seance, which was being held by a well-known medium who was visiting Glasgow. I was busy, so replied that I would not go. Later, however, I changed my mind. My brother told me that he had been invited to this seance by a Glasgow Spiritualist, but that his name had not been mentioned. Consequently, we were going "incognito," which, he explained, would add greatly to the value of any evidence we might receive.

Arrived at our destination, in a part of the city with which we were both unfamiliar, we found ourselves among a company of some ten or twelve persons, all of them complete strangers to us both. I cannot remember exactly how many were there, but I do remember that in the party there were only three men—my brother, myself and another who, for the moment, I shall call Mr. A. We adjourned to a room with windows heavily curtained, and in the centre of the floor, surrounded by a circle of chairs, stood an aluminium trumpet.

It was explained to me that this was to be a "direct voice" seance, that is to say, the spirits who would manifest their presence would speak through the trumpet, which was shaped like a megaphone, and this would enable their voices to be amplified sufficiently for us to hear them distinctly. My attention was drawn to a narrow band of phosphorescent paint on the trumpet, so that its movements might be followed in the dark. I must have asked the question, "Who is going to move it?" because I remember being told laughingly that the spirits would move it all over the room, even up to the ceiling. They might even give me a playful tap on the head with it or beat time to the music on it. Altogether, for a novice facing his first psychic adventure with some degree of trepidation, the whole affair seemed uncanny and not without some grounds for suspicion as to its genuineness.

I was warned by the medium that on no account was I to touch the trumpet if it came near me. Of course I was completely ignorant of such things as "ectoplasm," "psychic rods" or any of the methods by which psychic phenomena are produced, but the medium lent point to what she had just told me by drawing down her blouse slightly and showing me a red weal on her skin, such as might have been caused by the lash of a whip. She explained that this was the result of somebody having pulled the trumpet towards him at a seance some weeks previously, and that she had been ill for several days after the incident had occurred.

I decided to leave the trumpet alone.

We then seated ourselves, the light was switched out, and the seance commenced. It began by our singing "The Lord's my shepherd, I'll not want." As the room was in pitch darkness there was nothing for me to look at except the narrow phosphorescent band on the trumpet, and after all I had been told about the antics this instrument might possibly play I watched it closely. Before the seance had started I had held it in my hand, in fact I had been asked to replace it on the floor only a moment before the light had been put out, so I knew it had not been " faked " in any way. But soon it began to move perceptibly ; first a slight tilt to one side, then back to its normal position again. Gradually this movement increased until it swayed back and forward a few times and then, as I watched it, it rose a little off the floor. By the time we had finished singing the last verse it had risen higher and moved towards one of the sitters, although, so far as I could judge, it would still be not more than a few inches above the carpet.

The Lord's Prayer was then recited, followed by the voice of a sitter who seemed to be inviting any spirit friends who were among us to manifest their presence. This was answered by a distinct sound, like a loud whisper, from the direction of the trumpet. The sound increased until a normal voice broke through and addressed one of the sitters by name. Evidently the owner of the voice was recognised, as a short conversation ensued between the sitter and the voice. Another voice followed, speaking to another sitter. And so the seance proceeded, the trumpet moving about the Circle in the direction of the person addressed.

After a little time it was suggested that we should sing another hymn, and it was during the singing of this that I suddenly became conscious that something beyond the ordinary was definitely taking place. So far I had been interested in the conversations with the unknown voices in a detached sort of way, but I was not prepared to take them too seriously. Now, however, something occurred which arrested my full attention and which I could not explain. The hymn chosen was " When He cometh, when He cometh, to make up His jewels." It seemed to be a popular hymn with those present, who sang it lustily.

Now, what I lacked at that time in knowledge of psychic matters I made up for to some extent in my knowledge of music. I have always been fond of music, especially choral singing, of which I have had a fair amount of experience. Not only had I been well trained under one or two good choirmasters, but I have trained choirs myself with some success at musical festivals. Thanks to a naturally quick ear I could usually detect if any member of the choir was singing out of tune. I mention this fact because of what now followed.

As we were singing this hymn a voice joined in which I was certain did not belong to any of the sitters in the room. It was a strong tenor, and it was singing the tenor part of the tune. As I have already said there were only three men among the sitters—my brother, myself and Mr. A. The voice was certainly not my own. It was not my brother's, who has no musical ear and could not sing either tenor or bass if he tried. That left Mr. A., who happened to be sitting next but one to me on my left-hand side. I leant over towards him

and distinctly heard him singing the *air* of the tune.
In any event his was a deep voice, not a tenor.
But still the tenor voice continued, and it came from
the direction of the trumpet which, by now, was
floating near the ceiling. There could be no possible
doubt about it ; the voice did not belong to any of
the three male sitters, and it was unquestionably a
man's voice. I do not for a moment believe it
could have been imitated by a woman. During the
second verse of the hymn Mr. A. stopped singing.
My brother was not singing. It did not take a
trained ear to note the fact that the ladies of the
party were carrying on by themselves. But still
the tenor voice persisted, and as I listened intently
I detected a slight " tinny " sound in it which
could only be explained by the vibration of the
metal of the trumpet.

Whatever else happened that afternoon I do not
particularly remember, but that voice took some
explaining, and explain it is just what I could not do.
Was it conceivable that a " dead " person could
possibly sing a hymn along with people on earth ?
It sounds a childish question to ask now, but that
is the kind of conundrum which puzzles the beginner,
especially one like myself who had been brought up
in the atmosphere of an orthodox Presbyterian
home. I had been taught, and had accepted,
the regulation ideas of heaven and hell, but beyond
that had given the question of death and the
hereafter not much thought. Of course, the Bible
tells us that there is singing in heaven. In fact,
it would almost appear that most of one's time
there is to be taken up with singing " Hallelujahs,"

but that is rather different from a dead person singing
" When He cometh " in a room of a house in
Glasgow !   And yet, when the hymn was finished,
one of those present claimed the singer as her son
and had an intimate converstion with him.

It made me think !

Not long after this incident I met for the first
time the medium who was the means of convincing
me, beyond all doubt, of the reality of spirit
communication. This was John C. Sloan, of Glasgow,
who at that time was about the zenith of his
mediumistic power. His story has been told already
in my brother's book, " On the Edge of the
Etheric," so I shall not repeat it here.   But I
would be doing Sloan less than justice if I did not
add my own tribute to his simple, honest and straight-
forward character. To imagine his indulging in any
kind of fraud or trickery is impossible. Owing to
his poor eyesight he seldom read a book or a
newspaper. He was far from being what is usually
meant by the word " intelligent." But he had the
kindest heart of any man I ever knew. Two or
three nights a week, with unfailing regularity over a
period of many years, friends and strangers—it
mattered not which to him—gathered in his little
sitting-room and held intimate communion with
their loved ones beyond the veil. And never have
I known him accept a single penny for his services.
" If it makes other people happy, that is enough
for me," he would say if anybody offered him money.
Such conduct is not what one would expect from
anybody who was deliberately setting himself out
to deceive his fellow men and women, and the

fact that his employer was a frequent visitor at these seances makes any such suggestion all the more ridiculous.

For more than four years my brother and I sat frequently with Sloan, sometimes along with others but often with only a shorthand typist to record what was said. Those occasions were not entirely spent in conversations with our friends who had passed on, although many of these conversations yielded remarkable evidence. Naturally, there were many questions which we wanted to ask, and we soon found that one of Sloan's " guides " was able and willing to satisfy our desire for information on the vitally important subject of life after death.

In my earlier book, " The Unbroken Melody of Life," I have recorded some of my experiences with this medium ; others I propose to record now, but from the point of evidential value I do not think any exceeds the incident I am now about to relate. It occurred at one of my earliest sittings with him, and, looking back now, I think I can safely say that it was that incident and its sequel which finally broke down the barriers of scepticism and convinced me that communication between the two worlds was a definite and demonstrable reality. I wrote this story down in full at the time, and it was subsequently included in " On the Edge of the Etheric." This is what happened.

There were about a dozen people present, and in the course of the seance, after Sloan had been in trance for a short time, the trumpet moved over towards me and tapped me on the knee. A moment

later a voice spoke directly in front of where I was
sitting, saying " I am Eric Saunders." I asked if
the voice was addressing me and it replied " Yes,"
whereupon I said that there must be some mistake,
as I had never known anybody of that name.
The voice was not very strong, so some person
suggested that we should continue singing, and
while we were doing so the trumpet kept tapping
me on my knee and then on my arm and shoulder.
This was so insistent that at last I said, " I think
we had better stop singing, as somebody is
evidently most anxious to speak to me." Again
I asked who it was, and the voice, much stronger
this time, repeated, " Eric Saunders." Again I
said that I had never known any person of that
name, and asked where I had met him. The
reply was " In the Army." I mentioned a number
of places, which came into my mind on the spur
of the moment, such as Aldershot, Bisley, France,
Palestine, etc., but I was careful to omit Lowestoft,
where I had been stationed for the greater part of
the war. The voice replied " No, none of these
places. I knew you when you were near Lowestoft."
I at once seized on the word " near " and asked
why he said " *near* Lowestoft," to which came the
reply, " You were not at Lowestoft then but at
Kessingland." This is a small fishing hamlet about
five miles south of Lowestoft, where I was stationed
during part of 1917. I then asked what Company
he had been attached to, and as I could not make
out clearly whether he said " B " or " C," I asked
if he could remember the name of the Company
Commander. The reply was " Macnamara." This

was the name of the officer commanding "B" Company at that time.

By way of a test I pretended that I remembered the man, and said "Oh, yes, you were one of my Lewis gunners, were you not?" The reply was "No, you had not the Lewis guns then, it was the Hotchkiss." This was perfectly correct, as the Lewis guns had been taken from us in April, 1917, and were replaced by Hotchkiss. I then asked him two or three leading questions, such as the name of my billet, which he answered correctly, and then Saunders said "We had great times there, Sir; do you remember the General's inspection?" I laughed and said that we were continually being inspected by Generals, and asked him to which particular one did he refer. He replied "The day the General made us all race about with the guns." This was an incident which I remembered well and which had caused a considerable amount of amusement among the men at the time.

He then told me that he had been killed in France, and I asked him when he had gone overseas. He replied that he had gone with the "big draft" in August, 1917. I asked him why he had called it the "big draft," and he said "Don't you remember the big draft, when the Colonel came on the parade ground and made a speech?" I remembered it well. A particularly large draft was sent out to France from the battalion that month, and it was the only occasion I can recollect on which the Colonel personally said good-bye to the men.

Saunders then thanked me for the gunnery training I had given him, and said it had been most useful to him in France. I asked him why he had come to speak to me, and he said " Because I never have forgotten that you once did me a good turn." I remember once putting myself to some trouble and sacrificing a Saturday afternoon's holiday in order to obtain leave for one of my gunners, owing to some special circumstance, but whether his name was Saunders or not I cannot say. At the end of our conversation, clairvoyants who were present described Saunders standing in front of me speaking and, with a smile, saluting me before he left us.

Now comes the sequel to this strange incident. About six months later I was in London and there I met, by appointment, the Corporal who had been my assistant with the light guns in the battalion at that time. I told him the above story, and asked him if he remembered any man named Eric Saunders. It must be remembered that I had been training gunners for nearly two years, at the rate of about a dozen a fortnight, and beyond putting them through their examinations and taking a general oversight of them, I had never come into such close personal contact with them as to know many of their names. The Corporal, however, was more with the men but he could not remember any of this name.

Fortunately, however, on this afternoon when he met me, he had brought with him an old note-book in which he had been in the habit of keeping a full list of men under training and other information. He pulled this out of his pocket, and together we looked back until we came to the

records of "B" Company during 1917. Sure
enough the name Eric Saunders appeared there,
followed by "f.q. August, '17," with a red ink line
drawn through it. The letters f.q. stood for fully
qualified, and although I knew the meaning of the
red ink line, I asked the Corporal what it meant
as I wanted to hear it from his own lips. He
answered, "Don't you remember, Mr. Findlay,
I always drew a line through the men's names
when they went away. This shows that Saunders
went out in August, 1917."

Unfortunately, I had not asked Saunders the
name of his regiment, and consequently we were
unable to trace his death, as the War Office, without
this information, was unable to supply any details
beyond the fact that over 4,000 men named Saunders
fell in the war. I should add that men came to
Lowestoft for training from all over the country,
so I had no record of the regiment to which Saunders
belonged.

The critic will find it very difficult to explain
away this incident. Nobody at the seance, except
my brother, knew me, but even although I had
been well known to all of them, how could anybody
have gained possession of this information? It
is inconceivable that Sloan, who had his daily
work to attend to, could possibly have done so.
Was it all in my subconscious mind, waiting to be
dragged out in some mysterious way at this
particular moment? That is equally impossible.
I did not know that Saunders had gone out in the
"big draft." Among the hundreds of men who
had passed through my hands for training, over a

period of about two years, is it conceivable that I should remember all these facts about this one unknown man, whose very name I could not recollect even when it was recalled to my mind? But even allowing that the entire incident was a remarkable case of telepathy, it has still to be explained how my subconscious memories were turned into a voice which spoke so loudly that it was heard by everybody in the room.

No amount of telepathy can do that!

CHAPTER V.

IN WHAT BODY DO THEY COME?

IF the incident which I have recorded in the previous chapter be accepted as genuine, the implications arising from it are obviously of the utmost importance. They revolutionise our conceptions both of death and of our conditions in the life beyond.

Clairvoyants saw Eric Saunders standing in front of me. Then Saunders still existed in bodily form. His conversation testified to the fact that his memory still persisted. His statement that he had come back to thank me for some kindness I had done him in the past showed that he still possessed the attribute of gratitude, possibly a certain degree of affection. Obviously, too, the very fact that he returned at all demonstrated that he had the ability and desire to do so.

We are thus faced with the proposition that we continue to exist in the after-life in a body similar in appearance to that which we possessed here on earth, and that we carry with us into the next stage of our existence the memories of our earth life, our affection for those we have left behind and the ability to give expression to our desires.

Orthodox religion makes no attempt to reach such conclusions. It preaches a doctrine of hope and belief, based on the theory that, because Jesus rose from the dead, believers will do likewise on the Resurrection Morning. Even on the assumption (and it is only an assumption ; the Church does not attempt to prove it) that between death and the resurrection the spirit exists in some other sphere while the body lies in the grave, Orthodoxy remains silent as to the nature and form of the spirit, while holding divergent views as to the locality in which it dwells during this period of time.

The Church of Rome teaches that it undergoes a course of purification and progressive growth in Purgatory. The Church of England, on the other hand, openly confesses that it does not know. In " Doctrine in the Church of England," issued by the Commission on Christian Doctrine appointed by the Archbishops of Canterbury and York in 1922, and published in 1938, the doctrine of purification and further spiritual progression after death is dealt with alongside what it terms " the more distinctively evangelical tradition of the faithful departed as being immediately in joy and felicity." It expresses its doubt as to which of these two doctrines is the one which God actually revealed to the human race by suggesting that " those who after death are awaiting the General Resurrection " may be in a place called " Paradise," and it closes its argument with the words " In the judgment of the Commission the Church of England deliberately leaves room for both views." The sorrowing bereaved are thus left to extract as much consolation from this self-confessed ignorance on the part of their spiritual leaders as they can.

5

Obviously one of these doctrines must be wrong. They cannot possibly both be right as one directly contradicts the other. If the departed spirit is immediately in joy and felicity, then no further course of purification is necessary, while, on the other hand, if this course is necessary and the spirit is still on the road of progress, it cannot have reached the state of perfection described as being "in joy and felicity." The Church of England does not know and frankly says so.

The Westminster Confession of Faith, on which the beliefs of the Presbyterian Churches are based, at least knows where it stands and says so without any equivocation. I quote the relative passage in full :—

Chapter XXXII.—*Of the State of Men after Death, and of the Resurrection of the Dead.* " The bodies of men after death return to dust and see corruption ; but their souls (which neither die nor sleep) having an immortal subsistence, immediately return to God who gave them. The souls of the righteous, being then made perfect in holiness, are received into the highest heavens, where they behold the face of God in light and glory, waiting for the full redemption of their bodies ; and the souls of the wicked are cast into hell, where they remain in torments and utter darkness, reserved to the judgment of the great day. Besides these two places for souls separated from their bodies, the Scriptures acknowledgeth none."

In the following Chapter, which is headed
" *Of the Last Judgment,*" the Westminster Confession
affirms with equal conviction that on the Last Day—

" . . . all persons that have lived
upon earth shall appear before the tribunal
of Christ to give an account of their thoughts,
words and deeds, and to receive according to
what they have done in the body, whether
good or evil. The end of God's appointing
this day is for the manifestation of the glory
of his mercy in the eternal salvation of the elect,
and of his justice in the damnation of the
reprobate, who are wicked and disobedient.
For then shall the righteous go into everlasting life and receive that fulness of joy and
refreshing which shall come from the presence
of the Lord ; but the wicked, who know not
God, and obey not the gospel of Jesus Christ,
shall be cast into eternal torments and be
punished with everlasting destruction from the
presence of the Lord, and from the glory of his
power."

That teaching, which is elaborated and
annotated by proofs in the form of Scriptural
texts in the Shorter Catechism of the Presbyterian
Churches in Scotland (and is specially marked as
being " prepared for the use of schools "), at least
leaves no room for doubt as to the ultimate fate
that lies before every member of the human race.
But while one welcomes such forthright
expressions of belief, one must surely be struck
by what appears to be the unnecessary amount of

labour and trouble involved in putting this scheme into execution. The Church of England's doctrine of "Paradise" is the refinement of cruelty, as the unfortunate individual, who presumably still retains the use of his intellect, is left in the throes of an agonising doubt whether, on the Last Day, he will be considered sufficiently good to be received into heaven or, alternatively, be condemned to spend eternity in hell. The Presbyterian belief, on the other hand, consigns the individual *immediately after death* to one or other of these localities, and then, on the Last Day, drags him out again to be judged and sentenced. Surely it would be more in accordance with the recognised practice of justice to do the judging and sentencing first, instead of going through the farce of a "trial" on the Last Day, which may well be, for all we know, a few million years or so hence, during which lengthy period the reward has been enjoyed or the punishment endured, as the case may be.

I know that many church-goers will say "Oh, nobody believes that sort of thing to-day." But why not? At the Reformation the Protestant Church discarded the belief in an "Infallible" Church and pinned its faith for the future on an "Infallible" Book. It maintains that, once and for all, God revealed Himself to the world in the pages of that book, and consequently it has no right to alter or modify any of the teachings which that book contains, and on which its faith is founded.

But the days are past when people only have the Bible read to them by priests and parsons, and are told what they must believe. To-day, they are thinking for themselves, and they are not so easily convinced that the Bible is quite so infallible as they were once led to believe. So they are asking questions, and the Churches are finding it a difficult matter to give these questioners satisfactory answers. The truth is that the good ship "Orthodoxy" is firmly stuck in the mud, while the captain and officers are frantically rushing about the deck giving contradictory orders. No wonder churches are emptying while the call to "Return to the Faith" falls on deaf ears. It is not that people are becoming less interested in religion; in fact I should say that most people are more interested in it now than ever before. But to-day they are not satisfied with mere faith—they want that faith supported by Facts.

Is it any wonder, then, that the orthodox churches are unable to bring comfort and help to those who have been bereaved, and whose natural desire is to know with some degree of certainty the nature of the life into which their departed friends have entered?

Man is a trinity, consisting of body, soul and spirit. His spirit, or mind, is the seat of his consciousness; the fountain head from which spring the thoughts which are the basis of his speech and actions. In other words the spirit, or mind, is his True Self. It makes him what he is, in character and personality. His soul, sometimes referred to as the spirit body, is that through which his mind functions and his physical body is the vehicle which enables him to contact physical objects in a physical world. The spirit body is the etheric counterpart of the physical body. It inter-penetrates that body, just in the same way as water interpenetrates a sponge. If you soak a sponge thoroughly in water, you still have the sponge, but every particle of the sponge contains water. So every particle of the physical body contains the corresponding particle of the spirit body.

When death takes place the spirit body is released from its physical counterpart, but it still retains its shape and features. The reason why it is invisible to normal physical sight is because it is attuned to a rate of vibration which is more rapid than the physical eye can normally distinguish. But the eye of the clairvoyant extends over a wider range of vibrations, so the spirit form which is invisible to us is visible to him. This will perhaps be more easily understood by the beginner if we think of our wireless sets. The atmosphere all around us is filled with vibrations of many different " wave-lengths." When we switch on our wireless set we hear, transformed into speech or music, the particular rate of vibration applicable to the station to which our set is tuned in. The millions of other wave-lengths in existence still surround us as before, but we remain unconscious of their presence. A clairvoyant may thus be likened to a wireless set which is capable of picking up two stations, compared with another set which can only pick up one.

But this separation of the spirit body from the physical body does not depend on death. For a time they can be separated during life. This can occur during sleep or while the individual is under the influence of an anaesthetic. It can also take place when a person is in a state of hypnosis. The following example is taken from " Phantasms of the Living," a book compiled by three of the leading members of the Society of Psychical Research, and was corroborated by the Rev. Stainton Moses, who is the person referred to as " Z " in the story.

" One evening I resolved to appear to Z at some miles distance. I did not inform him beforehand of the intended experiment, but retired to rest shortly before midnight with my thoughts intently fixed on Z, with whose rooms and surroundings I was quite unacquainted. I soon fell asleep and awoke the next morning unconscious of anything having taken place. On seeing Z a few days later I inquired " Did anything happen at your rooms on Saturday night ? " " Yes," he replied, " a great deal happened. I had been sitting over the fire with Mr. M., smoking and chatting. About 12.30 he rose to leave and I let him out myself. I returned to the fire to finish my pipe when I saw you sitting in the chair just vacated by him. I looked intently at you and then took up a newspaper to assure myself that I was not dreaming ; but on laying it down I saw you still there. While I gazed at you, without speaking, you faded away."

The spirit body is joined to the physical body by a cord, referred to as the " silver cord " in the Book of Ecclesiastes, Chapter 12, verses 6 and 7 " Or ever the silver cord be loosed, or the golden bowl be broken . . . then shall the dust return to the earth as it was, and the spirit shall return to God who gave it," This cord may be likened to the umbilical cord which joins the newly-born infant to the mother. Death, after all, is only a form of birth. Instead of the physical body being born into a physical world, the spirit body is born into a spiritual world. Once this cord is broken the spirit body can never return again to its earthly home. It then begins to function on another plane of existence, the vibrations of which are higher, or more rapid, than those which go to make up the plane of physical matter which we can see with our physical eyes. But as the senses of the arisen spirit are in tune with the vibrations of its new surroundings, just as we are in tune with the vibrations of our physical surroundings here, life to it is just as normal and real as it is to us in our every-day existence on earth. But, let me repeat, the individual remains unaltered. In form and features he is an exact duplicate of the body he has discarded. A moment's thought will convince us that, if this were not the case, it would be impossible for friends to recognise each other in the life beyond death, when they meet there for the first time.

The spirit body is controlled by the mind, which continues to function through it after it has parted from its physical counterpart at death. It is our mind which makes us what we really are, not in the physical sense but in the vastly more important sense of spiritual values. Love, sympathy, kindliness, or conversely, hatred, envy and selfishness—these and other virtues or vices form our character. During our life on earth we make ourselves what we are by giving expression to the desires of our mind, be they good or bad, and as the mind is not affected by the death of the physical body it follows that we carry these desires with us into our new life.

Consequently, in that life, as well as being the same in appearance, we are also the same in character and personality. We still possess the same ideals, the same desires; our outlook on life remains unchanged. If we have been of a loving and sympathetic nature here, we shall be the same there. If our thoughts and actions here have been selfish or unkind, they will be the same there. Death does not change the individual in the slightest degree. Beyond the fact that he has discarded the physical body he remains exactly the same person in every respect, as he was while on earth.

So, in answer to the question at the beginning of this chapter, " In what body do they come?" we say that they come in their spirit body, with memory, affection and desires, just as they were when we knew them on earth. Would we really have it otherwise? Your boy, who gave his earthly life in the war, is still the same boy as he was here, with all his faults and failings, his high spirits and love of life and enjoyment. He may perhaps have " gone the pace " occasionally and in some respects been not all he might have been, but can we really imagine that God will judge that young life, cut off before it had become mellowed by experience, and condemn it to an existence of everlasting punishment because of a few youthful imperfections? To any intelligent person such an idea of God is akin to blasphemy.

The greatest mistake the Church ever made, and still continues to make, is to teach that Man was born a sinner, and that unless he accepts the doctrines it propounds he cannot be " saved." Even the Church itself is beginning to wake up to the absurdity of such a creed.   At a recent Convocation of Canterbury, one of the Bishops of the Church of England proposed that the Baptismal service should be amended by the deletion of the words " Who, being born in sin and in the wrath of God . . ."   Can any sensible person really believe that a new-born babe is a sinner and only worthy to be the unconscious victim of the wrath of God !   No wonder an intelligent public refuses to listen to such stuff and nonsense. And it is as cruel as it is absurd, causing endless and unnecessary suffering to mourners whose hearts are already breaking, but who are still dominated by the superstitions of a by-gone age.

Spiritualists will have none of such rubbish. We know that man is surely, if slowly, rising to a greater knowledge and understanding of spiritual truths, not " fallen " through some mythical transgression in a mythical Garden of Eden. And his upward journey is but beginning.   Death can neither arrest nor retard it.   His consciousness of right and wrong is no part of his physical being, which is all that death can touch.   His road leads upwards, and before him lies the path of eternal progression which is open to every human soul.

CHAPTER VI.

PAST AND PRESENT.

IF we were to delete from the Bible all references to what is to-day known as Psychic Phenomena we should find that we had little or nothing left of any value in what remained. It has been well said that the Bible is a book which was written by Spiritualists for Spiritualists, and that consequently only Spiritualists can fully understand it. This is not so much a figure of speech as it may sound. From Genesis to Revelation we find a continuous record of visions, angel ministry, heavenly voices, clairvoyance and clairaudience, and numerous other forms of psychic intercourse between this world and the unseen realms of spirit.

The prophets, or seers, of the Old Testament were the clairvoyants and clairaudients of those olden days. If one of our modern mediums had lived 3,000 years ago she would not have been called a medium, she would have been called a prophetess. To-day, in the eyes of the Law of this so-called enlightened country, she is ranked as a rogue and a vagabond under the Vagrancy Act. She is liable to be arrested, to be fined, even to be imprisoned for no other crime but that she makes use of her psychic gifts. Three thousand years ago she would have been taken care of and given every

opportunity to develop and practise her gifts,
just as in the case of the boy, Samuel, who was
what we, to-day, would call a "promising young
medium." We read that he was "given to the
Lord" by his parents; in other words he was
placed under the care of an experienced teacher,
Eli by name, who taught him how to use his gifts
aright. As we would say to-day, he developed his
mediumship so that, in course of time, he might
become a seer or a prophet.

Dr. Alexander Cruden, the compiler of the well-
known Biblical Concordance, tells us that in the
Bible the verb "to see" not only refers to the
seeing of external objects but also to that
"supernatural sight of hidden things." "Whence
it is," he continues, "that formerly they were
called Seers who afterwards were called Prophets."
This comment, of course, is in accordance with the
verse in the Book of Samuel, which reads
"Beforetime, when a man went to inquire of God,
thus he spake; Come and let us go to the seer,
for he that is now called a prophet was beforetime called a seer"—and we may add, "is to-day
called a medium." In fact, the word Prophet in
the Bible does not denote one who foretells future
events, as it means in our language to-day. It
denotes one who possessed the psychic gift, that is
to say, a person who was a Medium. According
to Chambers' Encyclopaedia, "The chief function
of the Old Testament prophets was to guide the
Children of Israel by messages received from God.
They burst forth with spiritual utterances under
Divine influence."

Dr. Cruden also gives us this further illuminating item of information, " The prophets, at the time they were transported by the spirit, were sometimes agitated in a violent manner. They used strange and unusual gestures, signs and speech. These motions were called ' prophesying '." Only a Spiritualist can fully understand the true meaning of that statement. But if Dr. Cruden had lived to-day, and had been interested in psychic research, he would most certainly have worded the last sentence differently. He would have said, " These motions indicated that the prophet (or medium) was going into trance or under control," just as we are accustomed to seeing our mediums do in these modern days under similar conditions.

One of the most common forms of mediumship to-day is Clairvoyance, which is usually accompanied by some degree of Clairaudience. In the Bible this particular psychic gift is spoken of as the " seeing eye and the hearing ear." It is also referred to in the Book of Samuel as the " open vision." We read " The word of the Lord was precious in those days ; there was no open vision." That simply means, in plain English, that at that particular time there was a dearth or scarcity of suitably developed clairvoyant or clairaudient mediums, in consequence of which the spirit guides were unable to give the people the counsel and instruction they had been taught to look for from the Spirit World. Far from being forbidden to communicate with the Unseen, as some ignorant people assert to-day, the Children of Israel were told over and over again to " inquire of the Lord " ;

in other words, to go to one of their prophets (or mediums) and get in touch with the Spirit World through him.

It must be remembered that the word " Lord " in the Old Testament does not always refer to God Almighty. It is a word which is used very loosely all through the earlier books of the Bible, as a casual glance will show, but it is chiefly used to denote Jahveh, the correct Hebrew name of Jehovah, who was the spirit guide of the Hebrew race. Consequently, the phrase " to inquire of the Lord " simply means " to inquire of Jahveh." Here is a verse from the Book of Ezekiel which any Spiritualist will understand—" Then the spirit spake with me and said, go, shut thyself in thy house . . . and when I speak with thee I will open thy mouth, and thou shalt say unto them, Thus saith the Lord." We are not told who that particular spirit was, but the quotation serves to show that " the Lord " was the name by which he was to be known.

Again we read in the Book of Kings of a certain occasion when Jehoram, King of Israel, and Jehoshaphat, King of Judah, were in a great difficulty. The people were grumbling and discontented, and they did not know what to do. " But Jehoshaphat said, Is there not here a prophet of the Lord that we may inquire of the Lord by him ? " Then one of the servants of the King of Israel remembered a young man who possessed the psychic gift. To-day we would call him a medium, but in the words of the Bible " The word of the Lord was with him." So the two kings went and

consulted him ; in twentieth century parlance
they " had a sitting " with him. Fortunately,
it was a successful sitting, as it produced the desired
result. The name of that young man was Elisha,
who subsequently became one of the greatest
prophets, or mediums, of his day.

If that incident had happened to-day Elisha
would probably have been arrested under the
Vagrancy Act for " pretending to communicate
with the spirits of the dead," and the Kings of
Israel and Judah would also have been taken
into custody on a charge of " conspiracy." But
as the story is recorded in the Bible, and the incident
occurred about 2,600 years ago, it is accepted as an
act of divine intervention, and our legal
administrators reverently bow their heads in awe.

But " sittings," as they are called to-day, were
not only held in these olden times for some special
or particular purpose. It is clear that they were
also held regularly with one of the recognised
mediums of the tribe. The prophet Ezekiel gave
sittings to the Elders of the tribe of Judah. " As
I sat in my house and the Elders of Judah sat
before me " is a phrase we read more than once
in the recorded story of that medium's psychic
utterances. On one of these occasions we are told
that " The hand of the Lord fell upon me."
Whether this hand was a materialised hand, or not,
is not stated, but there does not appear to be much
doubt on that point, as it was substantial enough
to lift Ezekiel off the ground and hold him
suspended between the floor and the ceiling.
Then, in the 20th chapter of Ezekiel, we read that

" Certain of the Elders came to inquire of the
Lord and they sat before me." Here we have the
" inquiring of the Lord " and the " sitting "
coupled together. The story goes on to say
" Then came the word of the Lord unto me, saying
. . . thus saith the Lord, are ye come to
inquire of me "—the spirit speaking through the
mouth of the medium.

As I write these words I am reminded of the
days when, as I have stated in an earlier chapter,
my brother and I frequently sat with John C.
Sloan, the Glasgow direct-voice medium. Naturally,
there were many questions we wanted to ask.
After Sloan had gone into trance the voice of one
of his guides would speak, and he generally said
something like this—" Good afternoon, my friends,
are there any questions you wish to ask me to-day ;
if so, I shall be happy to answer them." " Are
ye come to inquire of me " would be the Biblical
way of making the same remark, but both mean
exactly the same. The prophets of those days were
the mediums of to-day, and only when that fact is
realised can the Bible be properly understood.

I have emphasised this point because, if we
were to delete from the Bible all references to
psychic phenomena, we must begin by cutting out
all the utterances of the prophets from Samuel
to Malachi, and when we have done that we can
then proceed to delete such stories as Jacob's
vision, the angel providing water for Hagar's child,
Samuel's appearance to Saul, the writing on the
wall at Belshazzar's feast, and a host of other Old
Testament narratives.

Then we shall need to turn our attention to the Gospels. An angel visits Mary before the birth of Jesus; a choir of spirit voices is heard by the shepherds; Moses and Elias appear on the Mount of Transfiguration in materialised form; angels strengthen Jesus after the Temptation and in the Garden of Gethsemane; and after his death he appears in various places and to various people in his spirit body.

Even then we are by no means finished. From the Acts of the Apostles we must eliminate all reference to " tongues of fire " and " rushing mighty wind," no more must we speak of people being " filled with the Holy Ghost." We must cut out the story of Stephen's eloquent discourse, obviously delivered under some form of spirit control; Paul's experience on the road to Damascus; Peter's deliverance from prison; spirit healing; spirit lights; spirit guidance; the story of Cornelius and Peter's vision on the house-top, to mention only a few.

From the Epistles we must remove all references to spiritual gifts; Paul's advice as to how a church service should be conducted; ministering spirits and clouds of witnesses; while the Book of Revelation will be reduced from twenty-two chapters to the size of an insignificant scrap of paper.

Every form of psychic phenomena recorded in the Bible is recurring in these modern days. The barrier between the seen and the unseen worlds is again broken down, and spirit voices are reaching us from those " realms supernal " in which so

6

many of our dear ones dwell. The visions of those realms which, throughout the ages, have been vouchsafed to prophets, seers and mystics, are to-day being experienced by modern men and women who possess the same gifts as they did. Those gifts remain constant ; it is for us to accept them, if we are wise ; or reject them, if we are foolish.

For nearly one hundred years messages have been pouring through from the Spirit World. Highly progressed spirits from the loftier spheres, with spiritual knowledge and understanding far beyond that of any Pope or Archbishop, have been instructing us in those things that pertain to our spiritual welfare. They have taught us what is our duty to God and our neighbour. They have warned us unceasingly that true peace on earth can only be won by true brotherhood among men, and that this much desired state of affairs can only be brought about by putting into practice the Divine Law of Love.

And it is Love which brings our dear ones back to us, to assure us of their continued interest in those they have left behind. They wish us to know that they are not " dead " but still alive and actively engaged in various forms of useful service. They want us to know that they are frequently with us in our home, the office, the factory or the street, that they can hear our conversation and see our actions. They bring us news of those who are far from home and assure us that they, in spirit, are watching over them and protecting them from danger. Throughout the world to-day tens of thousands of sorrow-stricken souls bless Spiritualism for the comfort it has brought to them in the hour of bereavement. They have heard the sound of the voice which is supposed to be still, many of them have actually touched the vanished hand. They no longer need to hope or trust in some far-off reunion, vaguely taught and vaguely understood. They know from their own personal experience that their loved ones have never left them, but that, from time to time, they may still speak with them across the borderline of their new life.

It was said of Jesus that, if all the things He did and said were written down, even the world itself could not contain the books that should be written. The same might be said of the mass of evidence for survival which is being received by all sorts and conditions of men and women to-day. Only a minute fraction of that evidence ever reaches the eyes or ears of the public. Any Spiritualist can confirm my statement that this evidence is being given in hundreds of Spiritualist Churches and meeting-places, as well as in private homes, in this country alone every day of the week. I can only speak for myself. Let me give you some of my own experiences.

As I write this my younger son, Clark Findlay, is serving "somewhere abroad" with the Royal Air Force. He left this country in May, 1941, and after being for a short time at Singapore he was sent to Burma. Shortly afterwards Japan entered the war and Burma was invaded. Now, I have been in Burma. I have actually stayed with relatives at the place where his unit was stationed. For five months I did not receive any word from my son, but day after day I heard on the wireless " The Japanese have heavily bombed an aerodrome north of Rangoon," or some phrase to that effect. I knew that my son was at that aerodrome. But through it all my wife, in the spirit world, kept reassuring me. " Clark is quite safe ; don't worry," was her constant message. Then Rangoon was captured by the Japanese and our troops were forced northwards into the mountains of Upper Burma. What had become of my son? I did not know, but still my wife kept telling me that there was no need for anxiety.

I must now shift the scene of this story to the Spiritualist Church in Kilmarnock, Ayrshire, which is near my home and of which I am the president. Every Wednesday afternoon and evening a few members gather there to receive messages from their friends in the Beyond. On Wednesday, 25th February, 1942—please note the date carefully— a member of our committee, who had been at the meeting that afternoon, rang me up on the telephone. She told me that my wife had spoken to those present, urgently asking that somebody would give me a message from her at once. The message was, " Tell my husband there is no further cause for anxiety. Clark is safe. *He is on the sea.*" I expressed my gratitude for the message, but I was quite unable to understand it. How could Clark possibly be " on the sea " when our Forces were being driven inland *from* the sea ? It seemed impossible. So I accepted the part of the message that said he was safe, and possessed my soul in patience until some further news was forthcoming.

That news came about two months later, in a letter written by my son from Calcutta. He told me that he had got away from Burma at the last moment, on Monday, 23rd February, *by sea*, although for security reasons he was unable to give any details of how this had been managed. February 23rd ! And two days later, on Wednesday, February 25th, that information was given by a medium, Mrs. Dowds, of Paisley, to a small gathering in Kilmarnock, Scotland, and duly passed on to me at my wife's request. I make no comment on this story. Let our critics explain it as they wish.

Here is another story of the sea, although in this case the circumstances surrounding it are of a much more pleasant nature.

Some years ago, during a visit to London, I had a sitting with Mrs. Hester Dowden. In the course of this my wife suddenly made the unexpected remark, " Norman is having the time of his life. He is at sea. How that boy loves the sea ! " This completely mystified me. Norman, our elder son, was then about 16 years of age and at that moment was, so I believed, safely at school in Scotland. I knew that at the school there was a company of Sea Scouts, of which he was a member, and that frequently they went out sailing for the day. But that is rather different from " being at sea." So I replied to my wife's remark by saying " Norman is at school. He can't be at sea." " Oh yes," she replied, " he is. I know, because I went with him and some other boys and two grown-ups to a large town, and I saw them go on board a boat." This was news to me. " How long ago was that ? "

I asked. " About two days ago," was the reply, " they are near their destination by now."

A few days later I had a letter from my son. He had had " a glorious time." Apparently the school authorities had bought a 30-ton ketch for the boys' training. It had been delivered at Aberdeen and a small party of senior Sea Scouts, with two masters in charge (one of them a retired naval officer), had gone there to take over the boat and sail it round to Burghead, on the Moray Firth, the nearest harbour to the school. The statement that they were then near their destination was correct, up to a point, but not exactly in the sense in which I imagine it was meant. When entering the Moray Firth the youthful mariners struck half a gale. The sails had to be lowered and the boat proceeded under the power of an antiquated motor-engine, which eventually broke down. All the boys were violently sea-sick, including the one who was acting as cook, but as nobody showed any signs of desiring to eat perhaps that did not much matter. Eventually they dropped anchor in Burghead harbour on the morning of the day following the sitting. Those of my readers who, like myself, are fond of the sea will agree that, to a schoolboy similarly minded, this would indeed be a " glorious time ! "

Perhaps I should add that the sitting in question was arranged by telephone, at about two hours' notice. Mrs. Dowden had no reason to know that I even was in London.

I see from my notes that my father also communicated with me at this sitting. He finished by saying that my father-in-law was also present and wished to give me his greetings. There is nothing evidential about this message, but I append it as a matter of interest. Mrs. Dowden, who receives these communications by means of automatic writing, then wrote as follows :—

"This is Fred Stoop, Nellie's father. I came to-day as a sort of surprise to you, on account of its being Nellie's special day (it was the anniversary of my wife's passing). I don't come often, but that isn't because I don't think a lot about you. I have Nellie with me now, of course, but she is in advance of me. She knew a great deal more about this life than I did. I was a bit blind about this sort of thing when I was on earth, and just accepted what I was taught. I would have fought you hard if you had pressed me about it, but now I give in. You were right. I just took what they told me and only thought about it on Sundays. I'm not going to say I was sorry to find I was much the same when I came here as I was before. I think, on the whole, I was glad, and very glad when Nellie came to join me. She is always trying to get me to communicate, but you know how it is, John, I am still busy and as yet I am not always inclined to come. I don't think I would speak to anyone but you."

These remarks expressed my father-in-law's attitude towards Spiritualism exactly. I knew the subject did not interest him, so seldom

mentioned it in his presence. He was a man for
whom I had a great affection. His life was spent
in the service of others. I am glad to think that
he is "still busy."

In the 2nd Book of Kings we read the story
of a most interesting psychic incident. Similar
incidents happen to-day. A certain man named
Hezekiah was ill—so ill that we are told he was
"sick unto death," While in this condition
he received a visit from the prophet, or medium,
Isaiah, who doubtless did all he could to comfort
him but was unable to hold out any hope of
recovery. "Thou shalt die and not live," said
the prophet. Isaiah left him, and while Hezekiah
prayed a strange thing happened. Before Isaiah
had reached the middle court of Hezekiah's house
a voice spoke to him. Our critics would probably
dismiss the incident, if it happened to-day, by saying
that the voice must have belonged to somebody who
was hiding behind a door, or that Isaiah only
imagined he heard a voice in his subconscious mind.
Spiritualists, however, know better than to say
silly things like that. They know from their
own personal experiences that the voice was
undoubtedly that of Isaiah's spirit guide. And
this was the message which the voice gave him—
" Turn again, and tell Hezekiah . . . I have
heard thy prayer, I have seen thy tears ; behold,
I will heal thee." Isaiah did not doubt for a
moment that the message was a genuine one,
so he did as his spirit guide told him, much to
Hezekiah's happiness and comfort. The story
even suggests that his spirit guide instructed him

as to what treatment should be applied to Hezekiah so that his health might be restored.

Spiritualists frequently receive messages of help and comfort from the Spirit World. Our departed friends are very near us ; they are just as interested in our affairs as they ever were when on earth. It is in no way extraordinary, in fact it is only natural, that they should wish to aid us and give us messages of good cheer whenever they can.

A few months after my wife passed on, my two boys went to a public school. As I drove away after seeing them safely there, leaving them looking rather forlorn on the door-step as they waved good-bye to me, I could not help feeling rather sorry for the two motherless youngsters left among strangers, in strange surroundings far from home. During the next two days they were much in my mind. Then, on the following Sunday, I attended the morning service in Holland Street Spiritualist Church in Glasgow. Although I was well known to the members of the church I was completely unknown to the medium who conducted the service. I had never seen her before and I have never seen her since. During her demonstration of clairvoyance she pointed to me and said ''There is a lady standing here who gives me the name ' Nellie ' and says she is your wife.'' I acknowledged the name as being correct. '' She sends you her love,'' continued the medium, '' and asks me to tell you that she has been with the boys ; they are both well and are settling down happily in their new surroundings.''

Many people would call that a '' trivial '' message. Doubtless it was—to them. But it

meant a lot to me.　I do not believe that God
ever intended that the ability to pass on words of
comfort from the Spirit World should be confined to
the Isaiahs of the world several centuries ago.
What happened then can equally well happen now,
but Spiritualists are the only people who know this
from their own experience.　Consequently it is
they alone who reap the benefit of this knowledge.
But it is there for all who seek it.

CHAPTER VII.

FURTHER EVIDENCE.

ON one of the first occasions on which my wife communicated with me after her passing, she said " I am going to try and give you as much good evidence as possible ; it will be of use to you." I must leave it to the reader to decide whether or not she succeeded. I have already given two instances in which she gave me information which was unknown to me, and could not be known to the medium, and I propose to give some further similar instances in this chapter.

But, first of all, let us face the question— if the information given was not known to either the medium or myself, and therefore could not have been given by either of us, by whom was it given ? In the case of direct voice communications, the voice speaks entirely independently of the medium, sometimes several feet away from where he is sitting. In cases of trance, however, the communicator speaks through the lips of the medium. Where the information given is not known to the sitter, any possibility of telepathy or the subconscious mind can be ruled out, and obviously if it is not known to the medium it equally cannot emanate from his, or her, own mind. On the other hand, the very fact that an intelligent message is given at all is proof that it must emanate from an intelligent source. And the only source of that nature which exists lies in the personality of a living, conscious and intelligent being.

We are thus forced to the conclusion that, where the information given is unknown to both medium and sitter, it must come either from some other person not present, but still living upon this earth, or else from some discarnate being to whom the information was, or could be, known. Some critics assert that the medium is able, in some mysterious way, to " tap " the minds of living persons at a distance, and thus convey to the sitter the knowledge they possess, whether they may be consciously thinking of the subject or not.

But surely the answer to that theory is, firstly, that, considering the hundreds of millions of people who live in the world with hundreds of millions of thoughts in their minds, it would be an impossible chance that the medium should invariably succeed in picking out of some unknown individual's mind the one and only precise item of information which happens to interest the particular sitter of the moment ; especially as, nineteen times out of twenty, the sitter is a complete stranger to the medium. And, secondly, that the intelligence which gives the message claims to be, and gives the name of, some friend of the sitter who has lived on this earth, who has passed on, and who frequently also mentions the names of mutual acquaintances, either dead or alive, whom he, or she, professes to know. It is inconceivable that all such complicated and personal information could be extracted from any earthly source outside the seance room.

This leaves us with the only remaining, and only reasonable, explanation, namely, that the communications come from those whom they claim to be, living, conscious beings who have lived on this earth but who are now in that further state of existence which surrounds us, although invisible to normal physical sight. To receive a message, then, from one who claims to be, let us say, my father, who tells me something I do not know, and which the medium cannot know, but which is afterwards found to be correct; and who at the same time mentions the names of people also unknown to the medium but known to both my father and myself—that, I maintain, is sufficient evidence to convince me that my father has survived death and that he is able, as opportunity permits, to communicate with me. And if my father, or other person, can communicate with me, then any other spirit, who has likewise passed through the change we call death, can similarly communicate with others on this earth, if opportunity be given them to do so. If communication is possible for one, it must be possible for all.

I shall now give one or two further examples of information given to me, which could not have been known either to the medium or myself.

I was sitting with Mrs. Helen Spiers in London when my wife spoke to me and, in the course of our conversation, said " I was with Arthur (my brother) last night at Middlesbrough." I knew that my brother had been speaking in the Town Hall at Middlesbrough the previous night, and it is quite possible that Mrs. Spiers also knew this, so, from an evidential point of view, the remark was of no value. At that time I had never been in Middlesbrough, so I asked my wife if she could describe the hall, which she did in some detail. I wrote these particulars down in my note-book. Then she said " Ask him what happened in the middle of his address." On being asked to explain this remark, she continued " While he was speaking somebody called out something. I didn't hear what it was. He stopped, and the man sitting beside him stood up and said something ; then people began moving about in the hall. What went wrong ? "

After the sitting was over I asked Mrs. Spiers if she had ever been in the Town Hall at Middlesbrough, to which she replied that she had been to Middlesbrough but never in the Town Hall there. Here I may mention that I knew the late Mrs. Spiers for many years, not only as a medium but as a friend, and I can safely say that any person who knew her as I did would never dream of accusing her of anything but absolute truthfulness and honesty. She was one of the best known mediums in this country for many years, and I never heard the slightest suggestion, in any quarter, that she was other than absolutely trustworthy. However, as she admitted having been in Middlesbrough, I am prepared to rule out the validity of the evidence contained in my wife's description of the interior of the Town Hall. But what about the incident which she said had occurred during my brother's address ? The fact that Mrs. Spiers had once been in Middlesbrough could not explain that, as she certainly had not been there at the time the incident took place. There was absolutely no doubt on that point, as on the previous evening she had fulfilled an engagement in London.

This is what my brother told me later.

Apparently some people sitting at the back of the hall were unable to hear distinctly what was being said. Somebody called out " Speak louder ; we can't hear." My brother had turned to the chairman who was sitting next him and said " I'm speaking as loudly as I can," whereupon the chairman had risen and invited those at the back of the hall, who could not hear, to come forward to some vacant seats in the front. It was their doing so which had caused the " moving about in the hall " to which my wife had referred.

Now, putting aside the part of the message dealing with my brother having been speaking in Middlesbrough the previous night, and the description of the Town Hall, which might have been known to the medium, this story contains five separate facts which could not have been known either to Mrs. Spiers or myself. The sitting took place at eleven o'clock in the morning. Mrs. Spiers did not know I was coming. Middlesbrough is 246 miles from London. Did some person telephone or telegraph all this information to Mrs. Spiers ? If so, why ? Until I get a satisfactory answer to that question, or discover some other method by which the medium could become possessed of the details of this incident, I shall continue to accept the reasonable inference that the information was given to me by the person who professed to give it, namely, my wife. To end this story I may add that, about two years later, I had occasion to visit Middlesbrough myself. I took with me a note of the description of the Town Hall, as given to me at this sitting. Fortunately, the building was open, so I went inside and checked the various items referred to. All were exactly as my wife had described.

While writing the account of this incident I am reminded of another occasion on which Mrs. Spiers played a prominent part in a message given to me by my wife. This time, and in a most unexpected way, she confirmed some information which I had received through two other mediums.

My wife passed on in July, 1934, and in the following February I was having a sitting in Glasgow with Mrs. Bertha Harris. My wife said to me that, since her passing, she had been resting, but that now she was ready to undertake some active work. There is nothing remarkable about that. Frequently, those who pass on are ordered by the spirit doctors on the Other Side to rest for a time, especially if they have come through a long illness, as the depletion of the physical body affects the spirit body which has to be restored to a full measure of health, just as an invalid has to recuperate for a time on earth. My wife told me that, now that she was fit for service again, she would like to take up healing work, especially among children. This was just what I would have expected as, when on earth, she had been specially interested in the healing side of Spiritualism, and she had always been devoted to children.

About a month after this sitting with Mrs. Harris I again spoke to my wife, this time in London through the mediumship of Mrs. Agnes Abbott. Almost her first words were—speaking through Mrs. Abbott in trance—" I have good news for you to-day; I have started the healing work I spoke to you about and I am working with Helen Spiers." My wife had known Mrs. Spiers on earth, but I had never heard her speak of her as a healer; in fact, although I had known Mrs. Spiers for a number of years I was not aware that she undertook this type of Spiritualistic work. So I replied that I was glad she was going to work with Helen Spiers, but that I did not know she was a healer. " Neither did I," said my wife, " until I came over here, but she is; she does quite a lot of healing work, and it is nice I am to be working with somebody I know."

Now, these remarks had not been prompted by me. I had made no reference to our previous conversation through Mrs. Harris on the subject a few weeks earlier, so her remarks through Mrs. Abbott were, in themselves, of some evidential value. But more conclusive evidence was to follow.

The following evening I was speaking to the Duchess of Hamilton, and in the course of our conversation she asked me if I could give her the address of Mr. J. B. McIndoe, who was at that time president of the Spiritualists' National Union. She told me that she wanted to write to him but had mislaid his address. I gave her the address but, at the same time, I said that if she wanted to

get in touch with him quickly she might try and
see him while he was in London over the week-end,
as he had told me only a few days before that he
was to be speaking in the Queen's Hall on the
following Sunday evening. The Duchess wished to
send him rather an important message, and she
asked me if I would deliver it to him verbally at
this meeting.

Now, I had not seen any of the Spiritualist
weekly papers that week and consequently did
not know who was giving the clairvoyance in the
Queen's Hall on that Sunday, but I promised
the Duchess to deliver her message to Mr. McIndoe,
and Sunday evening found me seated in the front
row of the area of the Queen's Hall, waiting for
the service to commence. The platform party
took their places ; Mr. George Craze, the president
of the Marylebone Spiritualist Association, under
whose auspices these great Spiritualist gatherings
were held every Sunday evening until the Queen's
Hall was destroyed in one of the bad air raids on
London early in the war. Following him on to the
platform came Mr. McIndoe and, to my surprise,
Mrs. Helen Spiers as clairvoyante.

Immediately the service was over Mrs. Spiers
came to the front of the platform and beckoned to
me, saying " Come round and see me ; I have
something interesting to tell you." Of course,
I was going round to the ante-room in any
case to deliver my message to Mr. McIndoe, and
after I had done that I made my way to the room
in which I knew I would find Mrs. Spiers.
" This is a surprise," she said, as we greeted each

other, " I've been meaning to write to you for the past few days to tell you that Nellie (my wife) is now helping my healing guide. She's tremendously keen." Remembering my surprise when I heard that Mrs. Spiers did healing work, I replied " But, Helen, I never knew you did any healing. Is this something new ? " " Good gracious, no," she answered, " I've done healing work for ages. I'm so glad to have Nellie working with me ; she seems specially interested in children's cases."

Was all this an elaborate piece of collusion on the part of the three mediums concerned—Mrs. Harris, Mrs. Abbott and Mrs. Spiers ? Such a suggestion is too fantastic to be worthy of a moment's consideration. Mrs. Harris could not possibly have known that I intended being in London a few weeks after my sitting with her in Glasgow, and, even if she had known this, she did not know that I would have a sitting with Mrs. Abbott. Then did Mrs. Abbott communicate with Mrs. Spiers ? In that event the Duchess of Hamilton and Mr. McIndoe must be cited as either conscious, or unconscious, participators in the conspiracy. I had not intended going to the Queen's Hall that Sunday evening. It was only when I was asked to deliver the message to Mr. McIndoe that I decided to attend the service there. I might easily have called a few minutes before the service commenced, seen Mr. McIndoe, and come away again ; in which case Mrs. Spiers's part in the plot would have been a complete " flop." And, let me repeat, I had not in any way prompted my wife, when sitting with Mrs. Abbott, to make any reference to her idea of taking up healing work. Her remark that she "had good news for me," and that she was "working with Helen Spiers" was entirely spontaneous.

The suggestion of collusion in this case is almost as ridiculous as that once made to me, in all seriousness, by an opponent of Spiritualism, namely, that somewhere there existed a central office in which was kept a kind of card-index containing all available information regarding people who frequented Spiritualist meetings, and that mediums consulted this before visiting any locality to give a demonstration of clairvoyance ! If that suggestion is put forward to explain the incident I have just related, the card-index must be of formidable size, as it obviously must contain a record of the intentions and doings of the dead as well as of the living, seeing that the information regarding my "dead" wife's activities came from her and not from me.

The dictionary defines the Latin phrase, *reductio ad absurdum*, as meaning "proof by demonstrating the absurdity of the contrary proposition." It is a phrase which Spiritualists might often use when stressing the validity of their claims !

I feel I must apologise to my readers for bringing my wife's name so frequently into these stories, but at the beginning of this chapter I stated that she had told me that she would try and give me as much "good evidence" as possible. I can therefore only record the facts.

A few weeks after her passing I was staying in the South of England. One morning I received a letter from my brother. He had been speaking in the City Hall at Newcastle-on-Tyne. After his address Mrs. Helen Hughes gave a demonstration of clairaudience. My brother's letter was hurriedly written, merely to let me know that he had received, through Mrs. Hughes, about a dozen messages from my wife, which she had asked him to pass on to me. None of these messages was what could be called " evidential," in the strict sense of the word, as the information they contained was known to my brother. Also, my wife had known Mrs. Hughes during her life on earth. The evidence lay in a very different direction and came to me in a most unexpected way.

About a week later I came up to London one day to keep an appointment, but when I arrived at my club I found a note awaiting me saying that the appointment was cancelled. Having nothing else to do that afternoon I rang up the secretary of one of the large Spiritualist societies, the London Spiritualist Alliance, and asked her if she could book me a sitting with one of their mediums. " I'm very sorry," was the reply, " but I'm afraid all our mediums are already fully booked for to-day." My disappointment must have sounded in my voice, because she went on to say " but if you care to ring up again in about an hour's time I'll see what I can do for you in the meanwhile ; I'll telephone one or two mediums and see if they are free." When I rang up again an hour later—at five minutes to two, to be exact—I was informed that a medium had been found who could give me a sitting at half-

past two. " I don't know much about her," the
secretary explained, " but I'm afraid it is the best
I could do at such short notice."

Accordingly, at two-thirty, I found myself in a
room with a medium whom I had never seen or
heard of in my life before. My name had not been
mentioned. The medium went into a state of semi-
trance and my wife spoke to me. She told me,
among other things, that she had spoken to my
brother " quite recently." I asked her where.
She replied " In a big town up in the North."
I then asked her if she could describe the hall in
which the messages had been given. To my great
surprise she replied " It wasn't in a hall; it was in
a small room—a cosy little room in a house."
She then gave me a short description of the room,
particularly mentioning a " polished table " which
had stood in it. " Arthur (my brother) sat on one
side," she said, " and wrote down all I said.
Helen Hughes sat on the other, opposite him."
I could not understand it at all.

The same evening I met my brother. When I
told him the story he elucidated the apparent
mystery by telling me that the messages he had
passed on to me in his letter had not been given
to him in the City Hall at the time of the meeting,
which I had taken for granted, but that he had
received them at a private sitting which he had
had with Mrs. Hughes the following day. This
sitting had been held in a small sitting-room in a
private house. My brother confirmed the description
of the room, as had been given to me through the
medium in London, and on my meeting Mrs. Hughes

a few days later she did the same, both of them remembering the " polished table " and the position in which they had been sitting at it, all as correctly stated by my wife.

Neither telepathy nor the sub-conscious mind theory can explain this incident. I was definitely told something not only that I did not know, but that I actually thought was wrong. As for fraud would any medium, after being given the clue of a " meeting " and a " hall," be so foolish as to insist that the incident she was pretending to relate had occurred in a " small cosy room " in a private house, not to mention venturing on a description of the room, which she would know I could subsequently check ? And every room does not contain a polished table.

As a final example in this chapter let me give one which consists of some information given by my wife, not to me, but to somebody else concerning me, which information could not possibly have been known to him or to anybody present at the time.

A relative had died, and I had travelled from my home in Ayrshire to Surrey to attend the funeral. I returned to Glasgow the following day, and that evening I attended a meeting of the committee of the Glasgow Association of Spiritualists. The president of the Association at that time, Mr. W. T. Shields, was present, and I spoke to him before and after the meeting. I stayed in Glasgow over-night and returned home next day.

That evening I was sitting alone in the drawing-room, reading the evening paper after listening to the six o'clock news on the wircless, when suddenly

I felt a severe pain in my right side. Thinking it might be muscular I changed my position, but the pain continued. I rose, and as I did so the clock on the mantelpiece struck half-past six. I walked about the room for a few minutes, hoping that the pain might wear off, but it rather grew worse.

I sat down again and tried to continue reading the newspaper. But it was no good. The pain became so bad that I realised something would need to be done about it. A few minutes before seven o'clock my mother, who was staying with me, came into the room. Immediately she had visions of appendicitis, nursing homes, operations, and so forth, and told me that I had better get off to bed as quickly as possible while she telephoned for the doctor. A few minutes later she came upstairs to my room to tell me that the doctor's number was engaged but that she would try and get through to him as quickly as possible. This she managed to do after about ten minutes' delay. The point I want to make is that my mother did not mention my sudden illness on the telephone *until after seven o'clock*. The reason why I emphasise this fact will be seen as the story proceeds.

Next morning Mr. Shields telephoned my house. My mother answered the call. His first remark was " I was sorry to hear last night that Mr. Findlay was ill. He seemed all right when I saw him at the committee meeting the night before. How is he this morning? " My mother told him that I was much better, that the doctor had just been to see me and that he no longer feared appendicitis. It was only after she laid down the receiver that it suddenly dawned on her—how could Mr. Shields possibly have heard of my illness? She had never thought of asking him that question! It is a good thing that my mother believed in the truth of Spiritualism, otherwise she might have been shocked had Mr. Shields given her the explanation which he subsequently gave to me.

On the night on which I took ill so suddenly Mr. Shields and a number of friends attended a direct voice sitting in Glasgow. The sitting commenced at seven o'clock. In answer to my question Mr. Shields assured me that everybody was present before seven o'clock and that the sitting commenced promptly, or at the latest within five minutes of that hour. Among the first to communicate was my wife who spoke to Mr. Shields. She had never known him, so she introduced herself by saying " I am Mrs. Findlay." Now, Mr. Shields knew another Mrs. Findlay who had also passed on, so he asked which Mrs. Findlay was speaking. " I am Mrs. John Findlay," was the reply, " the wife of Mr. Findlay of your church." She then proceeded to say that she was very anxious about my health ; I had just taken ill ; she was afraid it was serious. Would Mr. Shields please let me know that I must take things more easily, as I was run down, etc. Her final words were " Do, please, tell him to be more careful of his health ; he is doing far too much."

Where did all this information come from? Remember, my mother did not telephone the doctor until after seven o'clock, by which time the sitters for the seance had all assembled. No person had left my house between six-thirty, when I took ill, and seven o'clock. I live in a country house, a considerable distance from any other dwelling, twenty-three miles from Glasgow. If that message was not given to Mr. Shields by my wife, I must leave it to our critics to say by whom it was given, and explain how. And let our critics bear in mind that it was no " illusion " on the part of Mr. Shields. The message was heard by everybody present in the room, and the door was locked.

In the incidents which I have related in this and the previous chapter there are no fewer than 30 separate facts given which could not possibly have been known to the medium and were certainly not known to the sitter. I am, of course, not including the story I have told regarding my wife doing " healing work," as that comes under a different category altogether. But as regards the others ; if the member of our church committee knew on that Wednesday afternoon that my younger son had escaped from Burma and was safely at sea, why did she not ring me up at once and tell me so ? What had she to gain by concocting a pantomime whereby the message would appear to come through the lips of a medium ? What had the medium to gain by being a party to such childish deception ?

The same applies to Mr. Shields. If he, or anybody else at the direct voice seance, knew that I had suddenly taken ill—although that knowledge could not possibly have been obtained in any normal way—why did they not say so, instead of producing an elaborate fake ? Mr. Shields certainly had nothing to gain by such a course of action, and who among the sitters, including the medium, would have dared to imitate my wife's voice? Any one of those present might have met her when she was on earth, as she frequently attended seances with me in Glasgow. If the information was imported from outside, who turned it into the voice which was heard by everybody in the room? And how was it done? Common sense dictates the only reasonable answer. Prejudice and bigotry may say what they like, but to any fair-minded person who is prepared to consider the matter dispassionately that answer is, that the so-called " dead " are still very much alive, that they are still interested in our affairs, and that, when opportunity permits, they and we can still communicate with each other across the narrow borderline which separates their world from ours.

CHAPTER VIII.

OUR CONTACT WITH THE SPIRIT WORLD.

SO far I have only dealt with a number of isolated instances of evidence which I have received, but it would be wrong to assume that all sittings produce a continuous stream of highly evidential information.

Mediums are like a telephone exchange. When it is in perfect working order messages can pass through it from one speaker to another clearly and correctly. But sometimes the junction between the two wires at the exchange is faulty, in which case the words spoken into the telephone at one end are not properly received at the other.

In the case of communication between us and those in the Spirit World not only has the possibility of a faulty " exchange " to be borne in mind, there is a further complication which renders it more difficult still. When somebody speaks to us on the telephone he is, at least, speaking to a person who is living on the same plane of existence as himself. His vocal organs vibrate the same atmosphere which, through the diaphragm of the receiver which we are holding in our hand, is again vibrated in the proximity of our ear.

But the communicators in the Spirit World are living on a different plane of existence. They may speak as loudly as they can, but the vibrations they thus cause have no effect on our normal organs of hearing. The medium must therefore act not only as an " exchange " but as a " transformer " as well, picking up the message on one wave of vibrations and passing it on, on another. The communicators, also, must bring themselves within the surroundings of the medium and sitter, and as the rate of vibration of their etheric bodies is different from ours, before they can make contact with us they must bring these vibrations into harmony with physical conditions. This is done by a conscious act of will on the part of the communicator ; in other words, by thought. The communicator *thinks* himself into physical surroundings and finds himself there.

We cannot fully understand this process until we realise that the Spirit World is a world of thought. We create our surroundings there by our thoughts. It seems absurd to say that we do the same here, but actually that is the case. Let me give you an illustration.

Let us suppose that you decide to build for yourself a new house. What do you do ? First of all, you decide the kind of house you want—large or small, approximately the number of rooms you will require; a bungalow, a house of two stories, perhaps even of three, and so on. You make these decisions as a result of your thoughts. You then put these thoughts on a piece of paper in the form of writing and you take the piece of paper to an architect, who reads it and thus transfers your thoughts to his mind. He then knows what kind of house you are thinking of building and this enables him, in his turn, to think out the details.

After his thoughts have reached a certain stage he sits down with his pencil, ruler and paper, and puts his thoughts into the form of a plan which corresponds as nearly as he can make it with what he knows your thoughts on the matter are. When his plan is completed he brings it to you for your approval. Probably you may think that a certain alteration would be an improvement, so he alters his plan by putting your thoughts into it instead of his own. Finally, the plan is passed as correct. The architect then gets in touch with the builders, the joiners, the plumbers, the electricians, none of whom can do anything towards their particular part of the work without giving the matter careful thought. They must think how much material and labour will be required, what these will cost, how long the work is likely to take, and so forth. In other words, the whole process of building the house, from the moment the idea entered your mind until the day the house is completed, is based upon *thought*.

You must think before you can act. The well-known saying, " He spoke without thinking," is untrue. It is usually spoken by way of excuse for some inapt remark, but to express the idea correctly we should say, " He thought wrongly before he spoke." You cannot speak without thinking any more than you can act without thinking, because thought is the basis of all speech and action.

I have shown how, in this life, we must think before we can build a house. But our thoughts would not build the house by themselves. We must have the assistance of the architect, the builder, and all the other people who help us to transform our thoughts into something tangible. But in the Spirit World these helps can be dispensed with. There, we are dealing with a substance that is more plastic than physical matter ; so plastic, in fact, that we can mould it into any shape we desire by our thoughts.

So when I say that the Spirit World is a world of thought, I mean that there we can create what we will by our thoughts. "As a man thinketh so he is." That is true, even in this life, although it is not always apparent to the onlooker who does not see the real individual, but only his physical counterpart. But when we reach the Spirit World we find that we have left this physical counterpart behind us, so we can camouflage ourselves no longer.

The same form of analogy applies to our method of locomotion in the Spirit World. Here, if we decide to take a journey, the process again commences in our thoughts. We then translate these thoughts into action by going to catch a bus or a train which takes us to our destination. But in the Spirit World buses and trains are unnecessary. If we decide to go on a journey there, we simply think of ourselves as being in the place we wish to be and find ourselves there.

I was given an example of this one day in London, when I had arranged a sitting at the London Spiritualist Alliance for 2.30 in the afternoon. While I was lunching in my club, my cousin and a friend came into the dining-room and sat down at a

table near one of the windows. After I had
finished lunch I went over and spoke to them for a
few minutes. Then I left to keep my appointment.
It was a very foggy day, so I decided to go by
underground instead of by bus or taxi.

During the course of the sitting my wife said
" I was with you while you were having lunch
and saw Erskine and somebody else come into the
room. They went to a table near a window and
you went over and spoke to them. Who was his
friend? I didn't recognise him." I gave her the
name of my cousin's friend and told her that I
did not think she had ever met him, although she
seemed to remember having heard his name. Then
my wife said " I followed you downstairs and saw
you put on your coat, but when you got outside I
lost you. Everything seemed suddenly to get
thick; you just disappeared." I replied that it
was a very foggy day and that possibly that
explained why she had not been able to see me out
of doors. "Anyway," she continued, " it didn't
matter. I knew you were coming here, so I just
came by myself, and was waiting for you on the
doorstep." I could not help being amused at this
simple and common-sense way of getting over the
difficulty, so I said laughingly " How did you come,
by taxi?" "Certainly not," she answered, " I
don't need anything as slow as that now. I just
thought myself here, and here I am." She finished
this part of the conversation with the remark,
" When you come over here there's a lot I can
teach you. We can do lots of things here that
you can't do."

Those, then, who wish to communicate with us from the Spirit World must first bring themselves into our physical conditions by the process of thought. This alters, or lowers, the vibrations of their spirit bodies until these become attuned to the vibrations of our physical world, just as we tune in our wireless sets from one station to another. They are then able to sense their physical surroundings.

But if communication is to be successful a further indispensable element is essential, namely, harmony of thought between the sitter and the communicator. The chemical constituents of oil and water have no affinity with each other, consequently they cannot mix. Similarly, the sitter attracts into his surroundings only those spirits whose mental outlook is of a like nature to his own. This brings me to say a few words about that mysterious part of us which is known as the aura, and few people realise what an important part this plays in our every-day life.

The dictionary defines the aura as " an invisible light which surrounds the human body," and up to a point that is correct, but the definition is not complete. The aura certainly does surround the human body ; it is also invisible to the average individual, although it is not invisible to the clairvoyant. But it is much more than that. In fact, every human being possesses two auras, quite separate and distinct from one another. One of these is known as the physical, or fixed, aura ; the other is termed the psychic aura ; it is also spoken of as the " mental " aura, because, as we shall see, it belongs to, and forms part of, the mental side of our nature.

The physical aura projects all round the body to the extent of roughly about an inch. To a clairvoyant it has much the same appearance as if a person had painted his body with luminous paint, which emits a faint glow. In the Book of Ecclesiastes it is referred to as "the golden bowl" (chapter 12, verse 6). This aura plays an important part as the means whereby we absorb into our bodies what we call vital force or energy. The atmosphere around us is full of this energy, which is continually being poured upon us from the sun. We absorb it through our physical aura. It flows through our nervous system just as blood flows through our veins and arteries. When a person is in perfect health he has an ample supply of this force; in fact, he has a super-abundance of it so he gives off what he does not require himself into the atmosphere. He hands on, so to speak, the surplus to other people. We speak of such people as "radiating vitality" to those around them. That is no mere form of speech; it is literally true. These people radiate vitality just as a flower radiates its perfume.

Similarly, a person who is forced to lead a sedentary life, and consequently has not the opportunity of enjoying a sufficient amount of fresh air and exercise, is frequently deficient in this vital force and absorbs it from those with whom he comes in contact. Some of us may have experienced this ourselves. We have felt an unaccountable weariness or tiredness after being

for any length of time in the company of some
particular acquaintance. The reason for this is
easily explained. That particular person has been
feeling run down, or for some reason lacking in this
vital force for which our physical bodies are
continually craving, and unconsciously he has
acted on us like a sponge—absorbing *our* energy
into his own system.

Some years ago, after undergoing a serious
operation, various circumstances conspired to
prevent my regaining my normal health as rapidly
as I should have done. At length I gave up dosing
myself with tonics and " pick-me-ups " and put
myself into the hands of Mr. Horace Leaf, a well-
known psychic healer. After a few weeks of his
treatment I felt so much better that I said to him
one day, " I wish I had come to you long ago ;
I feel a different person to what I did a month ago."
He laughed as he replied, " You don't need to tell
me that. I know it. When I started to treat you,
you nearly drained me dry ; I felt washed out after
I was finished with you. You are not taking a
quarter of the power out of me now that you did
then." In that case I was the " sponge," absorbing
the healer's vitality into my own system and thus
building up my bodily health.

But the aura which affects conditions between
the sitter and the communicator is not the physical
aura but the mental or psychic aura, which is part
of our spirit body and is of as much importance to the
spiritual side of our nature as the other is to the
physical. In order that we may understand the
appearance of this aura, as seen by a clairvoyant,

let us imagine the human body completely
surrounded by, and encased in, a globe of light.
This light extends all round the body—above the
head, below the feet, in front and behind and on
either side.   The body can therefore be likened
to a gold-fish lying in the centre of a glass bowl
filled with water which completely surrounds it
on every side, the water taking the place of the
aura, which streams forth from the body in
innumerable rays.   These rays are in a state of
constant vibration ; they change colour, expand or
contract, in sympathy with whatever emotion may
affect the individual at any particular moment.
Consequently, by means of the colour and formation
of the aura a clairvoyant is usually able to form a
correct idea of a person's mental outlook at any
given time.

For example, a person whose predominating
characteristic is that he is of a jealous or envious
disposition displays to the vision of the clairvoyant
an aura which is mainly green in colour.   " Green
with envy " is a common phrase, although few
people may know its origin.   Grey denotes fear,
and as long as the fear lasts the aura remains grey.
Red denotes anger, but if anger should give way to
blind passion, when we say that a person has
" lost control of himself," the aura resembles
nothing better than clouds of black smoke issuing
from some burning house, with tongues of livid red
flames darting through them.   On the other hand a
person who is in a state of spiritual ecstasy, or
labouring under some high resolve or emotional
upliftment, will show an aura of pale blue, pink, or a

delicate shade of yellow, possibly even a touch of mauve, which is one of the most beautiful colours an aura can show, denoting deep spiritual power.

And so throughout all the various ranges of emotion. Each one betrays itself in the aura, either by a change in its colour or in its formation.

In her book, " Man's Latent Powers," Miss Phoebe Payne, who herself is a clairvoyante, describes the aura thus :—

" As seen by the trained clairvoyant the aura shows a series of concentric rings of different densities of matter, varying widely in size and colour according to the evolution of the person. The general effect is that of an oval cloud of rapidly-vibrating multi-coloured mist, of which the dense physical body forms the core. Both the colouring and the shape of the ovoid change incessantly according to the play of mind and emotion, producing a kaleidoscopic display. The quality and tone-range of this colourful aura are determined by the nature of the thought and feeling with which they are connected. As an illustration, a research student constantly working upon an elaborate and exact scientific formula will show an aura which tends to a precise demarcation of mental from emotional matter. The colouring may not be vivid, but it will be clear and arranged in patterns, which are likely to be sharply defined and in accordance with the nature of his thoughts. The aura of an artist, on the other hand, is

usually brilliantly coloured, often without
definite design, but ebbing and flowing with
the play of his artistic conceptions in which
thought and emotion are inextricably mingled.''

It will thus be seen, as I have already stated,
that the aura gives an indication of a person's
temperament and character. But what I want to
emphasise at the moment is the *effect* which our
aura has, not only on ourselves but on other people
with whom we come into contact every hour of the
day. Because it has an effect and a much more
important effect than many of us perhaps imagine.

How often do we take sudden likes and dislikes
to people at first sight, without being able to explain
why? From the first moment we meet a person
we instinctively feel that he can be our friend
or, conversely, that he is a man we would not trust.
We go into a room, perhaps, and see a stranger
there. Before we are ever introduced to him we
feel that we are either attracted or repelled by his
presence. Many of us must have had this experience.
The reason is this. We do not need to come within
hand-shaking distance of a person before we actually
meet him. As our aura projects from us, so his
aura projects from him, and the two auras meet
midway between us. If we are both like-minded,
if our thoughts, ideals and emotions are in harmony
with each other the two auras dovetail into one
another. On the other hand, if we are spiritually
and emotionally antagonistic the auras clash, like
a wave flinging itself against a sea wall. They are
thrown back on themselves, and this produces,

through our etheric body, a sensation of dislike which is immediately transmitted to our brain.

Now let us go a stage further. The physical aura dies with the physical body. The psychic aura passes on with the spirit body into the Spirit World. Over there it is just as real, just as important, as it was here. The fact that it has shed the physical envelope which contained it during earth-life does not alter it in the slighest degree. We frequently hear people complain that they never succeed in getting a message from their spirit friends when they sit with a medium. They say " I go to this meeting or to that ; I have sat with this medium or that one, but I never seem to get a message." There may be many reasons for that, into which I need not enter now, but I can give one of them. If a sitter's thoughts are filled with selfishness, anger or bitterness, he is creating around him an aura which the spirit people cannot penetrate —at least, not the spirit people he wants to contact. Like draws to like. Evil attracts evil just as good attracts good. The man of angry, bitter or vengeful thoughts attracts angry, bitter and vengeful spirits, in precisely the same way as the high-minded and spiritual man attracts spirits of a higher order. And they make contact with each other through the aura—the aura of the discarnate spirit harmonising with the aura of the spirit still in the physical body.

The late Mr. Frank Blake told me of an interesting, if rather terrifying, experience he once had, which may help to illustrate my point. He had been conducting a service in a Spiritualist

Church a considerable distance from his home, during the course of which he had given a demonstration of clairvoyance. It was a wintry night, cold and wet, and he still had before him a two hours' journey by train. When he reached the railway station he found that his train was not due for another three-quarters of an hour, so he decided to try and find some place where he could have some supper. The station was in a poor quarter of the town, but he remembered having passed an hotel of sorts a short distance along the street.

Accordingly, he set off to find it. There was a strong wind blowing, with heavy rain, and holding his umbrella in front of him he mistook the building he came to, with the result that on opening the door of what he thought was the hotel he discovered himself in what he tersely described as a " low-class pub." However, thoughts of comfortable quarters and congenial company were of lesser importance in his mind than a strong desire for some form of food and drink, so he went forward to the counter, was supplied with what he wanted, and then retired to an empty table in a corner of the room. Only then did he begin to take stock of his surroundings.

" It wasn't the place itself," he told me, " or even the people who were in it, although they looked a pretty tough crowd ; but I was still partially under psychic influence after giving clairvoyance, and what I saw clairvoyantly almost frightened me." To his clairvoyant vision the room was filled with evil-looking, depraved spirits, who were trying to force themselves within the

auras of those who were standing at the counter,
drinking and swearing, so that they might in that
way participate to some extent in their sensations.
Some of these spirits were actually trying to grasp
the tumblers with their hands. They joined in the
laughter which followed each coarse jest. " I have
never seen such a terrible sight in my life," Blake
said, " and I never want to see another like it."

But he realised his danger. He knew that in
the semi-psychic state in which he then was he was
more than normally open to the influences by
which he was surrounded. " What did you do ? "
I asked. " I did the only thing I could do," he
replied, " I prayed for protection." " Yes," he
added, " and I got it. The spirits saw me all right,
but I saw myself surrounded by a circle of light ;
they couldn't get near me."

There is a lot to be learned from that story,
but apart from that it serves to illustrate what
I mean when I say that, to make a sitting successful,
the auras of both sitter and communicator must
harmonise.

Miss Dion Fortune in her book, " Psychic Self
Defence," says :—

> " Invisible forms move among us, whose
> actions we do not perceive though we may be
> profoundly affected by them. . . . Until
> the aura is penetrated there can be no entrance
> to the soul, and the aura is always penetrated
> from within."

That is a point we would do well to remember.
The aura is always penetrated from within. As a

man thinketh, so he is. One of the truths which Spiritualism is trying to impress upon the world is that of Personal Responsibility. We cannot shift that responsibility on to anybody else's shoulders. As we sow so shall we reap. "Sow a thought, reap a deed; sow a deed, reap a habit; sow a habit, reap a character." And character is the architect of the aura—character, the result of habit, of deeds and of thoughts. We cannot think evil without opening up a pathway through which evil spirits can find an entrance to our soul. Similarly, thoughts of kindness, sympathy and love towards all produce around us an aura which permits that inflow if Divine goodness which raises us to high and noble words and deeds. "The aura is penetrated from within." It is for us to decide what type of spirit we allow to penetrate it. The choice lies with us.

CHAPTER IX.

THE SPIRIT WORLD'S CONTACT WITH US.

IF Spiritualism did nothing more than convince people that the Spirit World exists and that human beings are in every respect the same individuals after passing through the change called " death " as they were before it, it would more than justify its existence.

It is really extraordinary that so much ignorance and complete lack of interest in the after-life should exist among so-called intelligent people. Heaven and hell, in the orthodox sense of the words, no longer mean anything to the ordinary man in the street. His ideas of what will happen to him after his life on earth is over are of the vaguest, ranging from complete extinction, on the one hand, to floating about space as an angel, on the other. Only those who have taken the trouble to inquire intelligently into the matter by studying psychic science have any definite knowledge on the subject. They know that the Spirit World, to which we pass when our earthly life is over, is really part of this world, and that passing into it does not mean separation, in the geographical sense, such as is implied in the well-known words, " There is a happy land, far, far away." These words, and others like them, sung and heard continually by successive generations of worshipping Christians, have given an entirely wrong idea of that world to which we are all travelling.

The close proximity of our next stage of existence is continually being stressed by those who speak to us across the borderline of death. They impress upon us that they are often with us, and that, by influencing us by their thoughts, they try to guide us aright in our words and actions. To give only one quotation—the communicator in " Children of Evolution " writes through the hand of his medium :—

" At every stage of his career man, whether he is aware of it or not, whether he wills it or not, is subject to strong influences from the astral plane. His every step on earth is watched over by kind friends in the spirit plane. There is as much interest taken in the humblest among you as in your most distinguished personages. No matter how insignificant by birth, position and attainments he may be, his career is watched with absorbing interest on the astral plane. He may be neglected, slighted, humiliated and insulted every day of his life, it makes not the slighest difference on this side. So long as you have breath in your bodies you have hosts of loving friends around you, endeavouring, often vainly, to help you on your way. No sickness or misfortune befalls you, but that every attempt is made to mitigate its effects ; in sunshine no less than in shadow we are with you with our good influence, endeavouring in every way to help you onwards."

Whether or not this close contact between the seen and the unseen worlds always acts on us for our good is a matter for us to decide.   We have been given Freewill, and that means that we are free to choose the kind of influence we desire.   We choose our unseen companions just as truly as we choose our friends on earth.   Birds of a feather flock together, we are told, and this proverb holds good whether we are dealing with beings who are discarnate or still in the physical body.   The mere fact that a person has shed his earth-body no more changes his character and outlook on life than does his changing from one train to another at a railway junction.   He continues his journey in the second train, but in every respect he is precisely the same individual that he was before the railway junction was reached.   Death does not change anybody into an angel or a devil.   If he was an angel in this life he will be an angel over yonder.   If he was a devil here he will still be a devil there.

But there is another aspect of this question which claims our attention, as its importance is not always appreciated as fully as it should be. In fact, among the great majority of people, whose knowledge of psychic matters is non-existent, it is not appreciated at all, because to them such subjects are as a book which has never been opened. Its contents are unknown.

It is well known that mediumship, or the psychic power, is frequently an hereditary gift. Among Spiritualists this gift is carefully tended. They know its value if properly developed.   They also know its dangers.   Some of my readers may be

surprised when I say that nothing can be more
dangerous than to be psychic, and not know it.
I do not say " is " but " can be." A great deal
depends on the individual concerned, but there
have been countless cases in which a person, unaware
of his psychic powers, has been the unconscious
victim of some discarnate spirit who has either
influenced his mind, or possibly taken control of
his physical organism and used it for his own ends.

What we are often inclined to forget is that the
Spirit World is inhabited by all sorts of people.
They go to that world from this one, so the various
types we find here are also to be found there.
The spirit message recorded by Dr. Funk in his
book " The Widow's Mite " puts it very neatly,
" Yes, we have many fools over here, but if you
continue to send us fools how can we help it ! "
When we hang a murderer we say, in our ignorance,
" Good riddance of bad rubbish." But that is just
where we are very far wrong. We only get rid of his
physical body, but the " bad rubbish " is in the man
himself, and all we have done by hanging him is to
send that bad rubbish into the Spirit World where,
if his mind is still intent on murder, he may easily
find somebody on earth whom he can influence to
carry out his nefarious design. Such people are
usually a nuisance to others when they are here ;
they are an equal nuisance over there. If only
they could be isolated like a person suffering from
an infectious disease their capacity for making
trouble would be limited, but the tragedy is that
in so many cases they are " earthbound " and still
endeavour to interfere with matters on this material

plane, sometimes with distressing if not disastrous results.

"As the soul lives on earth," says Imperator in "Spirit Teachings," "so does it go to spirit-life. Its tastes, its predilections, its habits, its antipathies, they are with it still. It is not changed save in the accident of being freed from the body. The soul that on earth has been low in taste and impure in habit does not change its nature by passing from the earth-sphere, any more than the soul that has been truthful, pure and progressive becomes base and bad by death. The one is no more possible than the other. The soul's character has been a daily, hourly growth. It has not been an overlaying of the soul with that which can be thrown off. Rather it has been a weaving into the nature of the spirit that which becomes part of itself, identified with its nature, inseparable from its character."

Some years ago, a man whom I had known died after a very short illness. I was from home at the time and consequently did not hear any particulars of the cause of his death. Poor fellow! If ever anybody made a thorough mess of his life, that man did. I must be careful what I write, but although I shall alter names and omit some details the material facts in the story I am about to tell are true in every respect.

About two months after his passing I attended the evening service in a Spiritualist Church in the South of England. I do not remember the name of the medium who gave the clairvoyance, but to be truthful I must say that I think I had met her before. However, although she may have known

something about myself, it is extremely unlikely
that she knew anything about my friends and
acquaintances.

During her demonstration she described in some
detail the figure of a man, corresponding very closely
to that of the man I had known, and stated correctly
his approximate age at the time of passing.
" He tells me that his name is James," she said,
" but that he was generally known by another
name." She then gave me another name—the
one by which I had known him. After I had
accepted this information she proceeded to tell me
the cause of his death. This was unknown to me,
but on making inquiries afterwards I found that
this was also correct. The medium then hesitated
for a few moments, and said " He seems to be in
great distress and is most anxious to give you a
message."

Knowing what I did of his history I could well
understand his being in a state of distress, so I
encouraged him by saying that I was glad he had
come to speak to me and that I would do my best
to help him in any way I could. " He wants you
to send a message to his parents," continued the
medium. I promised that I would do so. The
message was to the effect that he now realised what
a mess he had made of things. He was terribly
sorry and asked their forgiveness. He had been
in a dreadful state of mind since he had passed on,
as he saw the suffering he had caused and wanted
to put things right, but this was the first time he
had been able to contact anybody on earth who
had known him.

I knew that his parents were strongly opposed to Spiritualism, but I felt in honour bound to pass on this message to them.   I got no reply.

A few weeks later I was walking along Oxford Street in London when I unexpectedly met one of James's business associates.   I had no idea that this man was in any way interested in Spiritualism, so was extremely surprised when he told me that he had just come from having a sitting with a well-known medium, and that James had been urging him to do various things which he, James, had assured him would help to put matters right. We both agreed, however, that matters could not be put right quite so easily.   Broken hearts are hard to mend.

About two years later one of James's sons was visiting friends in Scotland, and I asked him to come and spend a few days with me at my home. I had never met him before, but found him a nice, straight-forward young fellow of about 20 years of age, keen on games but equally keen to get on in the world.   His father's name was seldom mentioned, and when the conversation eventually drifted round to Spiritualism I did not refer to the fact that his father had communicated with me. Bertie knew nothing about Spiritualism but took an intelligent interest in the subject, and I lent him one or two books to read.   I soon came to the conclusion, from the questions he asked, that there was something on his mind which he either could not, or did not like to, express in words. But at length it came out.   He frankly confessed that for some months he had been worried about

9

something which he could not understand. He did not know if it had anything to do with Spiritualism or not, but at any rate he had decided to take me into his confidence and perhaps I could explain the cause of his trouble.

And his trouble was this. In his bedroom at his home there was a wardrobe with a long plate-glass mirror. This stood against the wall opposite his bed, in such a position that when he sat up in bed he looked directly into the mirror. One night he had been reading in bed, and after laying down his book he happened to glance at the mirror before switching off the light. What he saw there gave him a shock. It was his father's face he was looking at, not his own ! He gazed at it for a few moments in bewilderment, but there was no mistake about it. He was not " seeing things ! " He jumped out of bed, crossed the room to the wash-hand basin where he sponged his face, dried it with a towel, and then looked into the glass on the dressing-table. His features were normal. So he decided to put the incident out of his mind and think no more about it. But he admitted that it had " shaken him up " a bit.

Not long afterwards the same thing happened again, this time as he was getting up in the morning. In fact, it had happened on several occasions, sometimes in this mirror and sometimes in others. As time went on he began to " sense " that his father's presence was beside him. This, he told me, made him feel restless and uncomfortable. I asked him if he had ever seen his father or heard his voice, but he replied to both of these questions in the negative. It was only after he had told me of these experiences that I remembered that there was a decided psychic strain in his family. I have already said that mediumship, or the psychic power, is frequently hereditary, and it seemed obvious that, in this case, Bertie possessed the gift to some extent without being aware of the fact. Small wonder, then, that these incidents had upset him !

But what disturbed me was the fact that his father was evidently trying to contact him in some way, and I had my reasons for being strongly of the opinion that this might not be altogether for the boy's good. Death does not change our character. We still possess the same desires after death as we possessed before it. And we still want to gratify them.

Two or three days later I came into the room where Bertie was sitting by the fire reading. I sat down to write some letters. After a while my attention was drawn to him because, every now and again, he drew his hand across his face, much as if he were brushing away a fly. I suppose it was the movement of his arm which caught my eye, but having noticed it I also saw that he was occasionally jerking his head or his shoulders, or shifting his position in the chair. This was so unlike the boy's natural behaviour that I deliberately watched him for some time while pretending to be absorbed in my letter writing.

Now, I know that I shall be accused of imagination, wishful-thinking, auto-suggestion and so forth, but I must risk that and say fearlessly

that beyond any shadow of doubt it seemed to me
that Bertie's features were changing their expression.
He was looking—in profile, as I was seeing him—
a much older man than his years.   I moved over
to the chair on the opposite side of the fire and said
" Well, Bertie, what's the trouble ? "   He looked
up, rather startled, and then in a rather shy,
apologetic sort of voice, he said " Oh, it's all right,
but—but it's father.   You know what I told you
about him.   I never felt him so close as he is now."

Beyond possessing some healing power I am no
more psychic than the average man, but we all have
a certain amount of it in us ; in fact, it is the psychic
power of the sitters, added to that of the medium,
which helps to produce the phenomena of the
seance room.   Was it possible, then, that *my*
psychic power, added to Bertie's, was enabling his
father to come so close to him that he was actually
trying to control his body ?   It rather looked like
it, and the idea of such a thing did not appeal to me.

I rose from my chair and stood in front of him.
I spoke, not to Bertie but to his father, and I spoke
plainly.   The fact that I did not see the person I
was addressing did not make my remarks any less
emphatic and to the point.   " Clear out of here
at once," I said.   I know I raised my voice, but I
was angry and did not attempt to disguise the fact.
" What do you mean by trying to interfere with this
boy.   Can't you see you are worrying him ?
What's your game ?   Do you want to take control
of him and drag him down to your level ? "
Anyone seeing me standing there, addressing what,
to all appearances, was nothing but empty space,

would be justified in thinking that I had taken leave of my senses! But I was certain that the boy's father was there. I had seen for myself the signs of intervention on the part of some spirit entity, and this had been confirmed by Bertie's own statement that he felt his father's presence very near him.

Looking back now on the incident I can laugh at the way I peremptorily pointed to the door as I bade this unseen intruder " clear out at once." Had I taken time to think I would have realised that neither doors nor windows were necessary to aid his departure! Whether my actions and my words frightened the father or the son I do not know, but a few minutes later Bertie assured me that his sensation of restlessness and discomfort had gone. Perhaps my scolding had had the desired effect!

But I was not content to let matters stop there. James, on earth, had been a man of strong and forceful personality. He had never been the sort of man who was easily beaten. Far from it. If he wanted anything badly he would go any length to get it. The fact that he had come back soon after his passing and had tried to urge one of his business colleagues how to " square up the mess " showed that he had not changed in that respect. Frankly, the matter worried me.

So, when I was in London a few weeks later, I called at the headquarters of one of the leading Spiritualist organisations, and there I had a long and confidential talk with a friend of mine who has had many more years of experience as a Spiritualist than I have. My idea was that if

Bertie could have a sitting with some medium, perhaps my friend, to whom I was speaking, would consent to be present, and if James manifested his presence I knew that my friend would know how to deal with the situation. To this my friend readily agreed and mentioned the name of a certain medium who, he said, was experienced in this form of work. He arranged to make an appointment with her through the secretary of the organisation without, of course, mentioning any names or imparting any information, and the following day I had word from him that a date for the sitting had been fixed. I wrote to Bertie, telling him what I had done, and advising him to keep this appointment, as I felt sure it would go a long way to putting an end to his trouble.

Later, after the sitting had taken place, I again called and saw my friend. He told me that after the medium had gone into trance her guide had announced that a spirit was present who wanted to know who " the stranger " was. My friend replied that, if the guide considered it advisable, he might allow this spirit to take control of the medium. This he did. At first the spirit, who said he was Bertie's father, was inclined to resent the presence of another person in the room, but my friend, with tact and knowledge born of many years of experience, gained his confidence and then explained to him the harm he might do his son by interfering with him as he had done. I need not repeat the conversation, but finally the boy's father had expressed his sorrow at what he had done and gave his promise that he would not do the same again. The sitting had ended with the medium's guide saying that he would do all he could to help James to make good the past and " see the light." I have met Bertie a number of times since then, and have always been glad to hear that he has never had any further experience such as I have described.

The 15th chapter of St. Luke's gospel contains one of the most moving stories in the Bible. A young man leaves his father's house, goes into a far country and wastes his substance with riotous living. And having come to the end of his tether he at length realises that he has made a fool of himself and decides to return home. His father sees him when " yet a great way off," and hastens along the road to greet him with an effusive and compassionate welcome. The story is a parable, symbolic of the welcome which the repentant sinner will receive from God when he turns from the error of his ways. I imagine it is the best known story in the Bible. Thousands of sermons have been preached on it.

But although there is no suggestion in the story, from beginning to end, that Jesus set a time limit on the son's return home, the orthodox churches emphatically affirm that such a time limit exists. They state dogmatically that only if the sinner repents and turns to God on this side of the grave will God have anything to do with him. Should he die unrepentant, or not have time to repent, he is eternally lost. In other words, the only period during which a sinner can be " saved " is while he is still alive upon this earth.

The Roman Catholic Church certainly holds out some hope for the future in its doctrine of Purgatory, a place in which the souls of the faithful are purified by suffering after death. The Protestant Churches, on the other hand, hold out no such hope. In the Westminster Confession of Faith of the Presbyterian Churches it is definitely laid down that, at death, the soul goes immediately either to heaven or hell, where it awaits the Day of Judgment at the end of the world. The Church of England is in two minds on the subject, some agreeing with the Presbyterian doctrine and others maintaining that the soul spends the intervening time in a place called Paradise. But whichever of the two may be correct, both are in agreement that after the Day of Judgment the individual who has done wrong on this earth is cast into hell and remains there for eternity.

In contrast to this the Spiritualist does not believe that it is only in this life that the sinner is given the opportunity to repent of his sin. Spiritualism teaches that there lies before every member of the human race a road of endless progression, that every chance will be given in the after-life to those who desire to make amends for the past, and that, if and when they decide to turn their thoughts to higher things, they will receive the assistance of bands of angel ministers to help them on their upward way. In this country the 7th Principle of Spiritualism reads " We believe in Eternal Progress open to every human soul." American Spiritualists phrase this slightly differently, " We affirm that the doorway to reformation is never closed against any human soul, here and hereafter." Both mean the same.

Both teach not merely the reasonable doctrine that a man should be given a second chance, but that God's love for humanity is such that He will give His children an infinity of chances, and that He will not be fully satisfied until the last and most obdurate transgressor finally returns from the far country into which he has strayed and is welcomed home into his Father's House.

There is another point in this story of the Prodigal Son to which I have never heard or seen any reference made by our orthodox spiritual teachers. " I will arise and go to my father," says the son, and this is immediately followed by the words " And he arose and came to his father." It sounds too easy ! If the story had been told in modern times one would almost imagine that the son had gone to the nearest railway station, settled himself comfortably in a first-class sleeping car, and arrived home in time for breakfast.

But the Spiritualist knows that the homeward journey would be far from being as easy as that. He knows that hell does not lie at the bottom of the downward path ; it lies on the road of the upward climb. There is no such place as a hell of ever-lasting punishment ; there is no room for such a place on the map of God's Universe. No matter how deep a soul may sink or how far he may go astray, somewhere, here or hereafter, sometime, sooner or later, like the Prodigal Son of old, he will " come to himself " and will arise and go to his father. But it will be a terrible journey—the long, slow, heart-breaking climb, back again up the hill down which he had slithered so easily, without thought of what lay at the bottom or how he was to get back to the top. Many a time will he lose his foot-hold, many a time will he go astray and have to start afresh, but eventually he must climb back to God at last. That is our true destiny, eternal progression, onward and upward through the spheres until at length we reach our goal, at-one-ment with the Divine.

The Christian Churches send missionaries to distant lands to convert the " heathen." Believing as they do, this is a praiseworthy object and for missionaries, as individuals, we can have nothing but the highest respect. But Spiritualists have missionaries too. They do not travel to distant lands because that is unnecessary, and they do not deal with souls incarnate on this earth but with those who have left this earth and are now inhabiting the World of Spirit which is all around us, although many of them are still in such a state of mental and spiritual darkness that they are actually unaware that they are dead.

Mr. Edward C. Randall, in his book " The Dead have never Died," recounts a conversation he once had with a " dead " man who was still in this state. This spirit had been a materialist on earth, having no belief in an after-life, and he was of the same opinion still. When Mr. Randall patiently endeavoured to explain to him the change that had taken place he angrily interrupted him, asking " What has all this got to do with me ? I am not dead nor am I interested in the subject."

Others again, and their numbers are many, realise that they have passed from this life, but they are dazed and bewildered, as the surroundings in which they find themselves are so completely different from what they had been led to expect. Those whose physical passions and desires were so strong that they had obtained the mastery over them remain earthbound in the company of others like themselves.   What greater punishment could be meted out to a man who on this earth was, let us say, cruel and selfish than to be forced to live continually with those who were as cruel and selfish as himself? Like draws to like, and in the Spirit World where our environemt is conditioned, not by the amount of money we have in the bank but by what we *are*, mentally and spiritually, we find ourselves in the place for which we are fitted as the result of the way in which we have lived our life on earth, and in the company of others like ourselves.

But such a condition need only be a temporary one. Few pass from this life without some knowledge of the difference between right and wrong, and once the liberated spirit puts forth a conscious effort to break from his surroundings and make progress, he immediately finds that effort meeting with success.

Some time after my wife's passing a certain lady whom we had both known also passed into spirit life. On earth she had been purse-proud, filled with an exalted idea of her own importance, and although she did many " good deeds " I must confess that they always appeared to be done chiefly for the purpose of gaining personal flattery and publicity. Shortly afterwards I asked my wife if she had met this lady since her passing. " Oh no," she replied, " she is not with us here. Her husband (who had also passed on) has not even seen her yet. He is very distressed about her." My wife went on to tell me that the person in question did not realise that she was " dead." She was continually in and around her earthly home and could not understand why some of the rooms were empty, while in others the furniture was covered with dust-sheets. She rang the bell for her maid and became angry when no maid appeared in answer to her summons. She wanted to know where all her servants were, why her family had stopped coming to see her and nobody took any notice of her. Mentally and spiritually that woman was precisely as she had been on earth, and for that reason she remained among the surroundings in which her sole interests lay.

At a later date, I am glad to say, my wife told me that certain friends in the Spirit World, herself among them, had been able to make contact with her and had helped her to change her outlook on life, with the result that she and her husband were re-united and she was once more a member of a happy family circle.

But there are many cases, alas, where the ministrations of spirit beings are well-nigh impossible. Their condition is, in some cases, so low that they are in actual fact nearer to this earth than to the world into which they have passed. That may seem a strange statement, but it will be understood when I repeat what I have already said, namely, that the vibrations of our spirit bodies are conditioned by our thoughts, and that the Spirit World itself is a world of thought. As we think, so we are. If our thoughts are depraved and corrupt our spirit bodies cannot be other than coarse and gross.

Such spirits can frequently be reached more easily by people on earth, and it is for this purpose that Spiritualists gather together in what are known as Rescue Circles. Those who attend these Circles are missionaries in the highest sense of the word. They must be spiritually minded to a high degree, so that their auras may not be penetrated by any of the undesirable influences which are bound to be present on these occasions, and they must have much tact and patience in handling those with whom they have to deal. Not many mediums are fitted for this class of work, which sometimes imposes a great strain on their physical organism, as it is usually necessary to allow the spirit to take control of the medium's body before any success can be obtained. The most widely known Circle of this description was that carried on in Buffalo, U.S.A., by Dr. Carl Wickland and his wife. For thirty years these two Spiritualist missionaries devoted their lives to rescuing souls in the Spirit World who were devoid of hope and seemed fated to spend years in misery and wretchedness of mind. Dr. Wickland's fascinating book, " Thirty Years Among the Dead," tells a revealing story of this most important work carried out by Spiritualists. Other records of similar seances are given in Admiral Usborne

Moore's "Glimpses of the Next State." Such Circles are common among Spiritualists throughout the world; to them and to those who take part in them many an undeveloped and backward soul, who has been condemned and forgotten by the world at large, owes his emancipation from a state of spiritual darkness and the commencement of a new and better life.

CHAPTER X.

THE CUMULATIVE VALUE OF EVIDENCE.

AT the beginning of an earlier chapter I said that it would be wrong to assume that all sittings produce a continuous stream of evidential information. But in many cases this does occur, although if notes are not taken at the time the facts given are likely to be forgotten, and in any event they are seldom made public.

The average person who sits with a medium, either privately or in what is termed a "Circle" or "Group" does not trouble to make any record of what takes place. Frequently the messages which the medium passes on from the discarnate spirit are by no means evidential, if judged from the standpoint of a critical investigator. But the great majority of these sitters are convinced Spiritualists, who have already received ample proof of survival and the possibility of spirit communication, and they attend these sittings solely for the purpose of retaining contact with some loved one who has passed on.

If we ring up a member of our family on the telephone for a friendly chat, we do not spend the time asking him for evidence that it is really he, himself, who is speaking to us, and not some stranger impersonating his voice and mannerisms.

The evidence comes out in the course of his conversation. I have frequently obtained the most convincing evidence outside the seance room altogether, in casual conversation with some medium who has passed on some message to me which she has suddenly received clairaudiently.

On one occasion, in a friend's drawing-room, with a number of other people in the room, a lady who was not a professional medium described to me the spirit form of an elderly man who, she said, was standing beside me. She told me that he was wearing an academic gown and hood. At the moment I could not think of any person to whom this description applied. She then said that he was telling her that he was my father's uncle and that his name was William. That piece of information enabled me to recognise him at once, and the message which the medium then gave me from him not only proved to be correct (I discovered this afterwards), but it was confirmed by my father, speaking to me through another medium at a later date. I should add that I had never met this lady before and that she knew nothing of any members of my family.

The investigator into Spiritualism is not likely to be convinced of the truth of spirit communication by attending one sitting or even two. After he has attended half a dozen he may, if he has been fortunate, have received some evidence which he cannot explain in any way except that the information must have come from the discarnate source purporting to have given it. But what our critics fail completely to take into consideration is the *cumulative* value of this evidence. They attend one or two sittings, or more probably they have never attended a sitting in their lives but have formed their conclusions on a few scattered experiences which they have read or heard of. And having carefully dissected each statement made, and discovered that there may be some loop-hole through which the information given might have been obtained by normal means, they at once cry "fraud" and dismiss Spiritualism as being unworthy of further consideration. As a lady once said to me on board ship, when I told her casually that I was a Spiritualist, "Well, I *am* surprised. My cousin once attended a Spiritualist meeting in London and he told me afterwards there was nothing in it. It is all hocus-pocus from beginning to end." I thanked her for this valuable contribution to the sum of human knowledge, but decided that I would preserve my own opinion on the matter, as I felt that possibly I knew more about the subject than she did—or even her cousin, in spite of his one visit to a Spiritualist meeting!

At a rough estimate there are about 1,200 Spiritualist churches in this country. Putting aside for the moment all week-day activities— and most churches hold meetings for clairvoyance and clairaudience on two or three occasions during the week—each church holds at least one service every Sunday. At this service a demonstration of clairvoyance and clairaudience is given, in the course of which not less than six—sometimes as many as ten—messages will be given to members of the congregation. Each message will contain, say, five separate statements which are either true or untrue. I am purposely placing these figures on the low side, and I shall continue this cautious estimate by allowing that half of these statements are not accepted as correct. From my own personal experience, however, over a number of years during which I have attended not less than forty such services each year, I would say that at least 80% of the messages given are accepted as correct.

But on the basis of 50% these figures mean that 18,000 correct messages are given by mediums every week at these Sunday services alone, to people who, in the vast majority of cases, they do not know and in whom they have not the slightest interest. These messages include descriptions of places or persons, Christian names and surnames, addresses, and in many cases the age of the person at the date of death and even the date of death itself. They include family matters, about which the medium could know nothing, information about absent friends or members of the family which is frequently not known at the time but confirmed as correct later. In short, they consist of information on all sorts of subjects which are of no interest whatever to the medium and which it would be a physical impossibility for him, or her, to acquire. And yet, our pompous critic, who has "once attended a Spiritualist meeting in London" is convinced that there is "nothing in it!"

Of course, in calculating this figure of 18,000 correct messages, it must be remembered that I am referring to one Sunday service only in each church. To obtain a more correct figure, account must be taken of the many churches which hold two or more services on Sundays, also of countless demonstrations given at other services held throughout the week or at private sittings or in groups. Then there are several thousand Home Circles throughout the country, the great majority of which meet once a week, the medium usually being a member or friend of the family. I have known of exceptionally good evidence being obtained at some of these homely gatherings, doubtless because the atmosphere is friendly and harmonious, thus creating the best conditions in which our spirit friends can draw near to us, and the medium can use his, or her, psychic power to the greatest advantage. And last, but not least, there are the many Psychic Research and Spiritualist Societies, where demonstrations of clairvoyance, clairaudience and psychometry are given to inquirers by a number of mediums every day of the week. Any person who cares to spend a few idle moments toying with figures will thus be able to obtain a rough idea of why I say that the cumulative value of evidence is a factor of importance well worth serious consideration before laying Spiritualism aside as being merely "hocus-pocus."

As an example of what I am sure every Spiritualist would call an evidential sitting, I cannot do better than include in this chapter an account of an experience which my brother and I had with Mrs. Bertha Harris a few days after our mother had passed on in February, 1936. This "sitting," if such it may be called, was in no way pre-arranged, and it was sheer good fortune that on the table beside the chair on which I was sitting there was a writing pad and that in my pocket there was a pencil. I was thus able to take full notes at the time of all Mrs. Harris said.

About a week after the passing of our mother, my brother and I motored in to Glasgow—some twenty miles distant from my mother's home, where we were staying at the time. While in Glasgow we called at the headquarters of the Glasgow Association of Spiritualists in Holland Street, and there found that a certain well-known medium had arrived that morning from the Midlands. My brother and I had both met this medium —Mrs. Bertha Harris—before, but we had no reason to think that she had heard of our mother's death. In fact, after making most careful inquiries, we are both convinced that it was virtually impossible for her to have known what had taken place in our family circle. In any event, as this record will show, she could not possibly have been aware of many items of information which she gave us on that occasion.

We had certainly no intention of having a " sitting " with any medium when we left home that morning, but as we sat in Mrs. Harris's sitting-room, engaged in general conversation, she suddenly turned to me and said " Mr. Findlay, your wife is standing beside you." As Mrs. Harris knew that my wife had passed on about eighteen months previously, and had in fact given me messages from her on more than one occasion, her remark, though naturally of personal interest to myself, was certainly not " evidence." But, after a short pause, she continued, " You both seem to bring an

atmosphere of sadness with you to-day. . . .
Some one has passed on within the past few days
. . . a lady, small, stooping slightly, about
eighty years of age I should imagine. . . .
Very closely connected with you. . . . Nellie
(my wife) brings her, but I cannot see her clearly;
I think she is finding it hard to show herself, but
Nellie is very distinct and she is smiling so happily."

By this time I had reached for the writing pad
which was lying on the table, and what follows is
taken from the notes which I wrote down at the
time.

Mrs. Harris—" Nellie is giving me the word
' Mother.' The old lady is either your mother
or her's. . . . She says she is *your* mother.
Have you lost your mother recently? "

We said that this was the case.

Mrs. H. (turning to me)—" The old lady speaks of
your birthday. She says you have not yet
bought the present she was giving you. It
was a book. She says she saw you take a piece
of paper out of your pocket in the book shop.
You were thinking of her at the time."

There are five facts here, all of which are correct,
and none of which could have been known to Mrs.
Harris. My mother passed on on 3rd February.
My birthday was on 19th January. When my
mother asked me what I wanted for a birthday
present from her, I had said I would like a certain
book which had been recently published. Owing
to my having had to go from home, however, I
had had no opportunity of ordering the book, but

a day or two after my mother's passing I wrote the title of the book, together with the names of author and publisher, on a piece of paper, and this I took out of my pocket in the book-shop and handed it to the assistant with the request that he would order the book for me.   Naturally, at the moment, my thoughts were centred on my mother. She had died after only two days' illness, and when she told me to get this book, only a fortnight before, I little thought that before I did so she would have passed on.

Mrs. H.—" Your mother says she had no feeling of surprise when she woke up on the Other Side —only one of great joy at seeing Robert again, and being able to hold his hand."

Robert was my father's name. He had passed on many years before.

Her remark about " feeling no surprise " is also quite understandable. Although not a Spiritualist, her views of death were fully in accordance with what we know to be the case.

Mrs. H.—" Your mother also mentions another Robert—not *her* Robert ; but an old gentleman who passed recently. He welcomed her, and is now looking after somebody else. She has also met Annie—a big woman ; a very old friend of her's."

The Robert mentioned was our uncle—our mother's brother-in-law. He had passed on about three months previously. The remark that " he is now looking after somebody else " is explained by the fact that his sister, Annie—a life-long friend of my mother—had also died, in Ireland, a few days before. Strangely enough, within twelve hours of my mother.

Mrs. H.—" Your mother is giving me the names 'Mary' and 'Elizabeth,' and sends them her love and gratitude. She says she has mentioned them both in her Will, giving them some recognition for all they had done for her. 'I always liked to pay my debts,' she says, 'and I have tried to repay them for all their kindness to me'."

" Mary " had been my mother's personal maid for over thirty years. " Elizabeth " was her cook, who had been with her for about twenty-seven years. My mother left each of them a legacy in her Will.

Mrs. H.—" She says that her last conscious memory of earth was Mary and Elizabeth standing beside her. 'Elizabeth,' she says, 'stroked my face with her hand.' Your mother says she was alone in the room with her at the time."

This incident was quite unknown to either my brother or myself, but on making inquiries we found it to be entirely correct. Mary and Elizabeth had been in my mother's room together, just about the time she lapsed into unconsciousness. Mary had gone into the dressing-room to get something, and while she was out of the room Elizabeth had stroked my mother's face with her hand.

Mrs. H.—" She wants you to thank Mary for
    placing the red flowers in her hand—afterwards.
    She says that red was her favourite colour."

This is correct.   Red was my mother's favourite
colour.   As for the rest of this message, which was
not known to my brother or myself, it appears that
my mother possessed some red artificial flowers
which had been given to her as a present by a dear
friend who had passed on.   After my mother's
body had been placed in the coffin Mary had
remembered these flowers and had placed them
in her hand.   I heard of this incident for the first
time when giving Mary my mother's message of
thanks.

Mrs. H. (turning to my brother)—" Your mother
    speaks of your daughter, young and tall.
    She was not able to come up to Scotland with
    you because she was away from home."

Correct.   When my mother suddenly became
seriously ill I telephoned to my brother, who lives
in Essex.   He and his wife at once hurried North,
but my niece was unable to accompany them as
she was from home visiting friends.

Mrs. H. (turning to me)—" Now she speaks of your
    two boys.   One of them—the elder—is about
    17, and tall for his age.   ' The other, I am still
    more concerned about.   Carry on what we
    thought best '."

I have two boys, the elder of whom was at this
time nearly 17 years of age.   For various reasons,
into which I need not enter here, my mother had

always been rather concerned about my younger boy's health.

Mrs. H.—" Your mother mentions various small gifts which she has left for different people. She says there are cards attached to each of them, bearing names and messages. (Turning to my brother)—She particularly mentions your daughter's gift as being a necklace."

This information was afterwards found to be correct, although it was unknown to either of us at the time. Only a few weeks before my mother's death she had gone over some of her possessions —jewellery, etc.—and had attached to each article to be given away, in the event of her death, a card bearing the name of the recipient together with a short message. The only person who knew that this had been done was her maid, and even she did not know what particular memento had been left to any particular individual. My mother's statement, therefore, that my brother's daughter was to receive a necklace is consequently all the more evidential as, almost certainly, no living person knew that this was the case.

Mrs. H. (turning to my brother)—" She says that she tried to keep her senses until you and Gertrude arrived, but that she did not succeed. You rushed up from a long distance. She kept thinking of your coming."

There is nothing particularly evidential in this message, except that the name of my brother's wife was given correctly. This might, or might not, have been known to Mrs. Harris, but as she had

only met my brother once before, and had never met
my sister-in-law, it is unlikely that the latter's
Christian name would be known to her. It is true
that my mother became unconscious about an hour
and a half before they arrived. Their " rushing
up from a long distance " refers, of course, to their
long journey, undertaken at almost a moment's
notice, from Essex to Scotland.

Mrs. H.—" Your mother mentions something in
    her bedroom which contains one small drawer.
    She is emphasising that—only one small drawer.
    In that drawer, she says, there are some old
    letters and papers that she knows will be of
    interest to you. She wants you to keep them
    and take good care of them. She is showing me
    a bunch of keys. I feel she wants me to say that
    one of these keys will give you access to this
    drawer."

This was one of the most evidential incidents
of the whole sitting, and deserves to be explained
in some detail.

Neither my brother nor myself could think of
anything in our mother's room which contained
only one small drawer. But, on our return home,
we went upstairs to her room to satisfy ourselves
on this point. As we expected, there was nothing
in the room which even remotely resembled anything
of the kind. Later in the evening, however, the
incident having meantime gone out of our minds,
we were discussing certain of our mother's affairs,
and a question arose which made it necessary for
something to be got from the wardrobe in her

room.   I ran upstairs and asked her maid to bring
the key of the wardrobe as I wanted it opened.
When I told her what was wanted, she at once
replied " Oh, yes, I know where it is," and opened
the wardrobe.

As she was getting the article for me I noticed
lying in the wardrobe a bunch of keys. Without
connecting this in my mind with what had taken
place earlier in the day, I picked it up and said
" Mary, what do these keys belong to ? "   She
took them from me—they were on a key-ring—
and said, holding them up one by one, " this is the
key of so-and-so, this is the key of so-and-so,"
and so on till she came to one small key, when she
said " and this is the key of your grandmother's
dressing case."   Then she suddenly seemed to
remember something, and added " Oh, that reminds
me, I forgot to bring it back after this room was
cleaned yesterday.   It's in the dressing-room."
And going into the adjoining room she returned with
a small oblong box of polished wood, which she
placed on the top of a chest of drawers. She then
explained that, before the bedroom had been cleaned
out the previous day, she had removed sundry
small articles into the dressing-room and had
omitted to return this dressing-case to its proper
place. As soon as I saw it I recognised it.   It had
stood on this chest of drawers in my mother's room
for years, but as it was always locked neither my
brother nor I had ever, as far as we can remember,
seen inside it. Neither of us knew that it had
once belonged to our grandmother, but this was later
confirmed as correct.

On being opened it looked just like any other dressing-case—some small receptacles for jewellery, trinkets, etc., and, round three sides, glass bottles with silver tops. I lifted one or two of these out and, as I replaced them, I was struck by something peculiar. The dressing-case was about five inches in depth, but the bottles were only about three inches in length, and they fitted into little hollows equally deep. I pointed this out to the maid and said "evidently this top tray lifts out. There must be something underneath." At the same time I ran my fingers round the edges, in order to get a hold on the "tray" to lift it out, when I suddenly touched a small knob. At the same moment a small drawer, actuated by a hidden spring, slid out from the bottom of the dressing-case. This drawer was filled with old family letters and papers.

My mother's maid was as surprised as I was at what had taken place. Of course, she knew nothing of our sitting with Mrs. Harris earlier in the day, but she at once exclaimed "I never knew that drawer existed—in fact, during all the years I have been with Mrs. Findlay, I never remember seeing inside this dressing-case before." On closing the small drawer we noticed that it was so constructed as to be practically invisible, unless one were deliberately looking for something of the kind.

So there was the object with "only one small drawer," and the "bunch of keys" contained the key which gave us access to it. Had it not been for our sitting with Mrs. Harris, and the information given to us through her by our mother, it is certain that that drawer would have remained unopened, and the letters and papers in contained —some of them of considerable interest—would still be undiscovered.

Mrs. Harris then proceeded to give an accurate description of the illness which had caused my mother's death. She referred to " weakness in the knees which made it difficult for her to rise." This is correct. Also, she said, " one of her eyes was very troublesome—not blind, but sore and uncomfortable. She keeps on doing this "—and Mrs. Harris wiped her right eye with her handkerchief. This is also correct. My mother's right eye had troubled her for some time, and she frequently used her handkerchief exactly as Mrs. Harris demonstrated.

After giving correctly the symptoms of my mother's last illness, Mrs. Harris added " She tells me that your father passed on as the result of something wrong here "—placing her hand over the appendix. This is also correct. My father died of appendicitis, twenty-nine years before my mother.

Mrs. H.—" She wants me to tell you that she has met Dr. Lamond. She says he looks younger now than she remembers him on earth."

The Rev. John Lamond, D.D., was a very old friend of my mother. She admired and respected him deeply. In his later years Dr. Lamond was a convinced Spiritualist, and actually gave up his charge of a large church in Edinburgh in order to speak on the Spiritualist platform. His name, therefore, was doubtless well known to Mrs. Harris, but it was surely a grave risk on her part to connect him so deliberately with my mother, on the remote chance that they might have known each other on earth. The sentence " He looks younger now than I remember him on earth " calls for no comment. It is in keeping with what we are told takes place after we pass into the Spirit World, namely, that the signs of old age soon fade from the features of those who have passed on.

Mrs. H.—" Your mother refers to a little old church she was fond of. There is something peculiar about the bell. Also she speaks of a Bible of her's which is in the church."

My mother worshipped in a very interesting and historic little church in the village near her home. It is bound up with the history of the Scottish Covenanters of the 17th century, on which subject my mother was somewhat of an authority. The church bell is certainly peculiar. It is not hidden inside a belfry, as is usually the case, but hangs on a little spire and is rung by means of a rope which comes down across the roof into the graveyard below. The person ringing it thus stands outside the church. As regards the Bible referred to, I think this was probably a French Bible which my mother always kept in her pew. My mother spoke French fluently at one time, and in her later years when she had not so much opportunity of doing so she kept up her knowledge of the language by reading in French. She kept this Bible, printed in that language, in church, so that she might follow the lessons in it as they were read.

Mrs. H.—" She sends her love to her two nieces, Margaret. One of them, she says, lives in Glasgow, the other near London."

This is correct. My mother had two nieces, both named Margaret. One lives in Glasgow, the other in Hertfordshire, not many miles from London.

Mrs. H. (turning to me)—" There is a coloured picture of your wife, your mother tells me, which stands on the narrow end of a piano, near the door of a room. The room has a high ceiling with a pattern on it."

Correct. A water-colour portrait of my wife stood on the end of the grand piano, just behind the door of the drawing-room in my mother's house. The ceiling of this room is a high one, and is decorated with a pattern.

In the foregoing narrative there are 43 separate facts mentioned which could not possibly have been known to Mrs. Harris. Many of them were not even known to my brother or myself. Where did all this information come from ? Who told Mrs. Harris that my mother had left a necklace to my niece ? Who told her of the existence of the drawer in the dressing case, and that in that drawer there was a collection of old letters and papers ? But it is idle to ask such questions. My contention is that the information given to us by Mrs. Harris on that occasion could only have come from one source, namely, from my mother who was the only person who had the information to give.

Rid yourself of the idea that my mother was "dead." She was not dead, and she is not dead now. She is much more actively alive to-day than for many years before she shed her physical body and passed into her present stage of existence. I watched her grow old, her face become wrinkled with age, her shoulders bent and her step slow and faltering. But when I saw these signs of old age I was not seeing my *real* mother, I was only seeing the physical body of which she was the tenant. To put the matter into every-day language, the tenancy of her physical home expired, so she left the house and went to live elsewhere. She did not take her furniture and her material belongings with her, but she took all that made her what she was to us, her sons, and to a host of friends—her personality, her character, her interest in people and things around her which persisted to the end of her earthly life. And she also took her memory with her, without which no inhabitant of the Spirit World could ever take the slightest interest in those they had loved and left behind. If that is her condition —if she no longer remembers me and others, and will not know us when we meet again, then, so far as I am concerned, she might as well be as lifeless as the paper on which I am now writing. Can any person imagine such a tragedy—to meet one's loved ones in the Great Beyond and find that they do not know you and have no further interest in your existence?

I maintain that this story which I have recounted proves beyond all question that my mother's personality still persists, that she still knows and remembers the people and incidents surrounding her life on earth, and, what is of far greater importance, that she is able to communicate, and has communicated, with us since she passed beyond our earthly sight.

CHAPTER XI.

STILL MORE EVIDENCE.

I DO not want to weary my readers by giving them too many examples of what are generally known as " experiences," but in writing this book I have set myself the task of recording proof that those whom the world calls " dead " are in reality very much alive, and that they are still interested in the affairs of those whom they have left behind on earth. My wife—I am sorry to bring her name in so often, but she plays just as important a part in this book as I do—told me shortly after her passing that she would give me as much evidence as she could to prove that communication between the two worlds is possible, so in fairness to her efforts it is only right that I should set down the information I have received from her from time to time.

To give anything like a complete record of all the many conversations I have had with her, and the numerous messages she has given me, would serve no useful purpose, but I now propose to recount a few further instances of evidence which is of value and which I have received, not only from her but from others. If my earlier remarks regarding the importance of cumulative evidence are correct then the more evidence I can produce the better. One of the secrets of good advertising is to keep hammering into the ears and eyes of the public the fact that *your* goods are the best on the market, and that nothing approaching similar quality can be got elsewhere. Well, I am out to " advertise " Spiritualism. I am out to spread the knowledge of the greatest truth the world can learn to-day—the truth that *there is no death* ; a truth which few people realise but which millions are aching to hear. And so the hammering goes on.

One of the arguments frequently brought against us by our critics is that so many of the messages received from the Other Side are " trivial " and consequently of no importance. That argument merely exposes the weakness of their case. What is a trivial message ? What may be a very trifling matter to an outsider may well be a definitely convincing item of proof to the recipient. And if our friends in the Spirit World did not speak to us about " trivial " affairs, what would our critics like them to speak about ?

I have several friends who have passed on and who communicate with me from time to time, but if any of them attempted to prove his, or her, identity by trying to expound, say, Einstein's Theory of Relativity or some equally abstruse problem, I frankly confess that the very fact of their doing so would be the first thing to make me doubt the genuineness of the message. Probably not one of them knew anything about this subject while they were on earth and cared less. Then why should they suddenly blossom forth as scientific experts merely because they have cast off their physical body and entered another realm of existence? But if these friends speak to me of some homely facts concerning their families or the every-day affairs in which they had been interested, surely such "trivial" communications are of far greater evidential value, especially if either known to me at the time or discovered later to be true.

The truth is that there are still many people who have the idea that when a person "dies" he is immediately transformed into some entirely different kind of being, endowed with unlimited wisdom and quite incapable of thinking, let alone speaking, of ordinary every-day affairs. To suggest otherwise is to "dishonour" the dead! To put it bluntly: if Tom Jones was Tom Jones on earth, speaking with a cockney accent and fond of spending his bank-holiday at Margate or on Hampstead Heath, he is still Tom Jones in the Spirit World, still speaking with a cockney accent, and I go so far as to say that, as likely as not, bank-holiday still finds him at Margate or on Hampstead Heath, enjoying the fun in the company of other discarnate spirits whose tastes are similar to his own. But if Tom Jones were to come back and speak to me in the accent of a B.B.C. announcer and tell me that he has no further interest in the gaieties of Margate or Hampstead Heath, that in itself would be enough to convince me that it was not Tom Jones who was speaking to me at all.

So, having cleared the ground, so to speak, on this subject of "trivial" messages, let us proceed with further evidence of the continuity of life beyond death, trivial though our critics may consider that evidence to be.

"RINGWOOD CALLING."

During a conversation with my wife through a medium in London, the medium being in trance, I suddenly said "Suppose we arrange a code-word between us ; then if I get the code-word from any medium I shall know you are there, even if you are not able to get through a longer message." My wife agreed to this and asked me to suggest a suitable word. On the spur of the moment I replied "what about ' Ringwood calling '." My only reason, I suppose, for thinking of this particular phrase was that my wife had passed on at Ringwood, in Hampshire, not long before, and in any event one phrase was as good as another. " Ringwood calling," repeated my wife, " yes, I can remember that easily." So we left it at that, and after the sitting was over the matter went out of my mind.

A few days later I acted as chairman at a Spiritualist meeting in Glasgow, at which a demonstration of clairaudience was given by Mrs. Helen Hughes. One of the disadvantages of being chairman on such occasions is that one seldom gets a message from the medium on the platform, but after the meeting was over Mrs. Hughes said to me " I almost gave you a message to-night, because your wife was with me all the time. She kept repeating " Tell him ' Ringwood calling,' ' Ringwood calling '; he knows what that means." That is

all she said." During the next few months I
received the same words through three separate
mediums in different parts of the country ; then the
story got into print, so I asked my wife not to use the
phrase again. From that day to this I have never
received that message from any medium.

"AN OLD FRIEND RETURNS."

In August, 1945, I had a sitting with Mrs.
Larder, of Birmingham, while she was visiting our
church in Kilmarnock. It was the first time I
had ever met this medium. In the course of the
sitting she suddenly said " A tall man has just
walked across the room and is standing beside you.
He is in naval uniform." Then she corrected
herself by adding " No, I do not think he is a sailor ;
he is wearing white trousers and a blue waistcoat
and jacket. Also a peaked cap. He looks more
as if he were dressed for yachting." As I had
known a number of yachtsmen who had passed on
this did not help me much, until Mrs. Larder
continued " He gives me his name as Dick
McCready." That was the last name I had
expected to hear and, although not exactly correct,
it was near enough. " He says," went on Mrs.
Larder, " do you remember the jolly times we had
sailing together ? "

Now, I had a great friend, Wycliffe McCready,
more intimately known as " Wyck," a keen
yachtsman, who was unusually tall. We sailed
together many times, not only in his own yacht

but with mutual friends. But the evidential point of this story is that *I did not know that " Wyck " McCready had passed on.* He was a big, strong fellow, and although I had not seen him for some years I had heard of him from time to time, retired from business and living in the country in Ireland. On making inquiries, however, I found it was true. He had died about a month before this sitting took place.

" MY MOTHER'S AUNT."

On Sunday, 24th May, 1936, I motored to Glasgow and attended the morning service at Holland Street (now St. Vincent Street) Spiritualist Church. As I sat among a large congregation the medium pointed to me and told me that there was a lady standing beside her on the platform who said she was my mother. She further informed me that my mother had brought with her " an old lady, an aunt, who passed on many years ago," and that the reason why she had brought her aunt was for the sake of evidence, as that day was the anniversary of her (the aunt's) passing. I replied that I knew my mother had an aunt who had died when I was a small boy, but that I was quite unaware of the date of her death. My mother then told me, through the medium, that I had in my possession a bundle of letters which had belonged to her, and that if I looked through this I would find a card giving the date of her aunt's death.

This was true. After my mother's death, about three months before, I had found a number

of letters in her writing-desk. These I had taken
home with me and put in a drawer, where they still
lay untouched. That evening I looked through
these letters and there found a card with a few lines
of poetry on it. At the top of the card was the
name of my mother's aunt and the date of her death
—26th May, 1895. But this message was given to
me on Sunday, 24th May. I was able, however, to
discover that in 1895 the 26th of May was a *Sunday*,
so that for all practical purposes my mother was
correct. The medium also told me that my mother
had had a great affection for this aunt, who had
been almost like a mother to her. This I knew to
be the case.

" THE ENGAGEMENT PRESENT."

On 28th May, 1935, I was present at a direct
voice seance with the medium John C. Sloan in the
house of a Glasgow lady, Mrs. Lang. Among those
present was the late Marchioness of Aberdeen,
who had never sat with Sloan before, and I was
told that he did not know she was to be at the
seance. I have beside me a typed copy of the
notes which were taken at the time by one of the
sitters. These are of considerable interest, but as
most of the conversation was of an intimate nature,
dealing with family matters and mentioning the
names of various relatives who are still on earth,
I cannot record it here.

Among those who spoke in the direct voice,
besides Lord Aberdeen, were the late Lord Rosebery,

Lord Goschen, Mr. Bonar Law and Mr. W. E. Gladstone. The last-named was an old family friend of both Lord and Lady Aberdeen, and he made a number of references to Hawarden which could not possibly have been known to the medium. One remark, however, I can record with safety. Lord Aberdeen was speaking, and said " Do you remember, Ishbel, the 25th of July ? That was a very happy day. Mrs. Gladstone sent you a picture." Lady Aberdeen told me later that this was a remarkable piece of evidence. The 25th of July was the date on which Lord and Lady Aberdeen had become engaged to be married. The same day they were driving down Bond Street in London together when they saw Mr. Gladstone on the pavement, so they drew up beside him and told him of their engagement. That evening Mrs. Gladstone sent her, by hand, a letter of congratulation, together with a small water-colour picture as a memento of the occasion.

Lady Aberdeen added that she did not think there was any living person on earth, except herself, who knew of this trifling incident.

" John Smith."

This incident also occurred at a direct voice sitting with John Sloan. Suddenly the trumpet tapped me on the knee and a strong voice spoke, " Mr. Findlay, I am John Smith from Darvel." Now, in this story I must use fictitious names. Some of those concerned are still on earth and, as

the story will show, it would be most indiscreet of
me to give any indication of their real identity,
especially as the town actually named is less than
ten miles from my home.

The name given by " John Smith "—his real
name—was unknown to me, so I replied " I am
Mr. Findlay, but I am afraid I cannot remember
you." To this came the answer " I never knew
you to speak to but I knew you well by sight, and
I'd be very grateful if you would do something for
me." I answered that I would. He then said
" I wish you would write to the Rev. Mr. ' Mackay '
in ' Darvel ' and ask him to tell my family that
I am not dead." " I'm *not* dead," he repeated in
a louder voice, " I never felt so well in my life."
He continued, " My family are mourning and
grieving for me. They think I'm dead. Tell
them the pain is all gone now ; they'll be glad to
know that." Then, after a moment's pause, he
added in rather a humorous tone " and when you
write to Mr. Mackay you can tell him I was standing
beside him when he buried my body in Darvel
cemetery three weeks ago."

I replied to this by telling "John Smith" that the
only difficulty I saw in delivering his message was
that I did not know if such a person as the Rev.
Mr. Mackay existed, but he countered that by
saying " Surely it won't be difficult to find that
out." So I promised I would do as he asked.

The following day I went to the Mitchell Library
in Glasgow and there obtained a copy of " The
Church of Scotland Year Book," from which I

found that there was a minister named " Mackay "
in the town of " Darvel." I at once wrote to him,
telling him the story as I have told it here, and
saying that I hoped he would see his way to pass
on the information to the man's family, as he was
obviously greatly concerned at their grief. By
return of post I received a reply. Mr. Mackay
told me that it was true that a member of his
congregation, named " John Smith," had died less
than a month before, that he had suffered a long
and painful illness, and that his family were in a
state of deep distress and grief. He also
corroberated Smith's statement that he (Mackay)
had conducted his funeral service in Darvel cemetery.
Every fact, therefore, given to me at the sitting
was correct.

Was it all a hoax? Had Sloan heard of this
man's death, and was he passing on all these details
to me for the express purpose of defrauding me?
At that time I had sat frequently with Sloan over
a period of about four years. He had never
attempted to trick me before; why should he
suddenly begin to do so now? Not for a moment
do I believe that Sloan was capable of any such
conduct. There were ten or twelve people present
at the sitting, any one of whom would have
recognised his voice, if it were Sloan himself who
was speaking. He was in trance at the other side
of the room, breathing regularly and heavily. The
voice spoke directly in front of me. Such an
elaborate piece of trickery on the part of Sloan,
for no purpose of gain but with grave risk to himself,
is unthinkable.

But I cannot end this story without quoting the last sentence in Mr. Mackay's letter to me. It was a perfect gem ! He wrote " But although what you tell me is true I would not think of giving this information to his (Smith's) family. *It might disturb their faith*." I refrain from comment on that truly priceless remark—beyond saying that, judging from the grief which this family was suffering, their " faith " did not appear to be doing them much good. Perhaps a little *knowledge* would have helped them.

" THE FORGOTTEN BIRTHDAY."

In September, 1938, I presided at a Spiritualist meeting in Kilmarnock, when a demonstration of clairaudience was given by a well-known Glasgow medium, Mrs. Edith Thomson. After the meeting was over, and before we had left the platform, Mrs. Thomson turned to me and said " Your wife is here ; she is telling me that you forgot her birthday last week." Only then did I remember that the anniversary of my wife's birthday had taken place a few days previously. I had to admit that I had forgotten all about it ! Mrs. Thomson went on, " She says she quite understands ; she knows you have been worried and anxious." Then, placing her hand over her appendix, she said " She tells me that her boy is ill. Is it appendicitis ? She knows that is why you forgot her birthday."

This was correct. My younger son had suddenly developed appendicitis and had been removed to a nursing home, where an operation had been performed. This, together with the fact that his sudden illness had disarranged my plans, was no doubt the reason why my wife's birthday had passed without my remembering it. There was nothing evidential in the remark about my son having appendicitis. Mrs. Thomson might easily have heard of that. But I do not know of anybody who could have told her the date of my wife's birthday, and, even if she had discovered that, how did she know that I had forgotten it ?

"THE MAN FROM JAMAICA."

In this story I play no part ; it was told to me by my brother.

Not long after his book, " On the Edge of the Etheric," was published he received a letter from a Mr. Nuttall, a lawyer in Jamaica, who was a complete stranger to him, saying that he had read the book and, as he was coming to England shortly and wanted to investigate Spiritualism, would my brother tell him the best way to go about it. My brother replied, advising him to get in touch with some of the well-known Spiritualist organisations in London, the names and addresses of which he gave him, adding that he would be glad to be of any further help to him, if necessary.

About three months later my brother received another letter from Mr. Nuttall, this time written from an hotel in London, asking him to come and have lunch with him. This my bother did. In the course of conversation Mr. Nuttall suddenly asked him if his wife had ever been in Jamaica. My brother replied that he thought she had, but that the visit must have taken place not less than twenty-five years ago. Mr. Nuttall then told him that at a certain sitting his father, who had been Archbishop of the West Indies, had spoken to him and had said " I must thank Mr. Findlay for being able to talk to you like this. I never knew Mr. Findlay but I remember once meeting his wife, although that was before she became his wife." He had then gone on to tell his son how, many years before, my sister-in-law's father and mother had visited Jamaica, accompanied by their then unmarried daughter, and that they had stayed with him there.

This, of course, was quite unknown to my brother, but on his return home he told his wife of this strange message, and she at once replied that it was correct. She remembered having stayed with the Archbishop and his wife, who were friends of her father, when she was in Jamaica with her parents before her marriage. At that time Mr. Nuttall had been only a schoolboy, and when my brother told him his wife's maiden name he had no recollection of ever having heard his parents speak of anybody of that name.

" THE WREATH."

In November, 1935, I had a sitting with Mrs. Helen Spiers in London. During this she said " Nellie (my wife) wants you to give her love to your mother. She is laughing and says that your mother is making a change in her household. She hopes the maid who is coming next week will be a greater success than the one who is going." These details regarding my mother's domestic affairs in Scotland, 400 miles away, were unknown to me at the time but were afterwards found to be correct. Whether or not the new maid was better than the old one I do not know, but that is no part of the story.

Mrs. Spiers then said " She is bringing with her to-day an old gentleman who is showing himself beside her. He is tall, and she tells me he is over eighty years of age. He has very recently passed over. I get the name Robert with him, also there is a John in spirit life, very closely connected to him." All this was correct. My uncle, named Robert, had died only a few days before. His son, John, had died about three years previously. Mrs. Spiers's description of my uncle's appearance was exactly correct, except on one point which I definitely thought was wrong. She said that he was " stooping slightly, and his chest was drawn in." I had not seen my uncle for some time, but he always held himself very erect with his chest rather " thrown out." I was told later, however, that during the last few months, in which he had grown very feeble, he had begun to stoop and this, of course, would cause his chest to appear " drawn in." Mrs. Spiers went on to say that he sent me his thanks for the " beautiful wreath " I had sent to his funeral. He especially liked the mauve background. What flowers were they ? " he asked, " they seemed an unusual kind."

Now, strange though it may seem, I could not answer this question. What had happened was this. I heard of my uncle's death just as I was leaving home, so I arranged with my mother that she would order a wreath to be sent from me, along with her own. Consequently, the design of my wreath and the flowers used in it were unknown to me. I saw my mother a few days later and, before telling her of my sitting with Mrs. Spiers, I asked her what sort of wreath she had sent from me to my uncle's funeral. She described it, saying " It was like a cushion ; the foundation was of *mauve* statice. . . . It looked lovely."

These incidents, together with others which I have recorded in previous chapters, are fair samples of the messages continually being received, either during the course of a public demonstration of clairvoyance and clairaudience or when having a private sitting with a medium. They are all what our critics call " trivial." But I submit that it is just because they are trivial that they are of value. Would Lady Aberdeen, for instance, have been more convinced of Mr. Gladstone's survival if he had given a political oration instead of referring to certain trivial incidents which took place during her visits to Hawarden ? And what could be more evidential than the trivial remark made by her husband that Mrs. Gladstone had sent her a picture on the day of their engagement ? " John Smith " was a plain man. If the minister, to whom I wrote, had had the courage to tell John's family that he had come back and spoken to me, would they have been more convinced of the fact that he still lived if he had assured them that John had delivered a weighty discourse (on some subject, presumably, of which he was probably entirely ignorant while on earth) rather than by his simple statement that " the pain is all gone now," that he was well and happy, and that there was no need for them to mourn his loss?   Mr. Nuttall's father was a man of considerable prominence in Jamaica, but what convinced his son was the trivial statement that he remembered meeting my sister-in-law there twenty-five years before.

Any one of these stories, taken by itself and critically analysed, may be found to be lacking on some point which precludes it from being classed as irrefutable evidence.   But considered as a whole, I maintain that the only reasonable explanation of the facts stated is that those purporting to give these messages actually did give them, thus demonstrating not only their survival of bodily death but that those who have passed on can, and do, communicate with us on earth.

If I were the only person to make this claim my testimony would be of little or no value. The stories I have related might well be dismissed as the product of imagination on the one hand, or a deliberate attempt to achieve cheap notoriety on the other.   But to my testimony, which can be confirmed by hundreds of thousands of other people in this country alone, must be added that of many eminent men and women throughout the world. People in outstanding positions, whether in Science, Law or any other branch of learning, do not make public pronouncements on matters of grave importance without carefully considering their words. No person in such a position would dare to express an opinion on the claims of Spiritualism without previously investigating thoroughly the alleged phenomena and satisfying himself that what he had experienced was genuine.

All the greater importance, therefore, must be attached to the words of a man such as Sir Oliver Lodge, F.R.S., who declared :—

> " I tell you with all the strength and conviction I can utter that we do persist, that people over there still take an interest in what is going on here, that they still help us and know far more about things than we do, and are able from time to time to communicate with us."

Another eminent scientist, Sir William Barrett, F.R.S., said :—

> " I am absolutely convinced of the fact that those who have lived on earth can and do communicate with us."

A generation earlier one of the greatest scientists of the Victorian era, Sir William Crookes, F.R.S., who commenced his investigations into psychic phenomena for the express purpose of exposing them as fraudulent, stated :—

> " To reject the recorded evidences on this subject is to reject all human testimony. No fact in sacred or profane history is supported by a stronger army of proofs."

Turning from Science to the Law, Sir Edward Marshall Hall, the famous King's Counsel, who directed his brilliant legally trained mind to this same investigation, wrote :—

> " I am convinced by things which have happened in my own life that there is survival after death, and means of communication with those remaining on earth. I have received time after time communications so meticulously accurate that it is impossible for any human being to have all the knowledge that these messages contain."

Distinguished people in other countries are no less definite in their testimony. Professor Hyslop, the American scientist, wrote :—

> " I regard the existence of discarnate spirits as scientifically proved, and I no longer refer to the sceptic as having any right to speak on the subject."

Camille Flammarion, the famous French astronomer, stated :—

> " I do not hesitate to affirm my conviction, based on personal examination of the subject, that any scientific man who declares the phenomena to be ' impossible ' is one who speaks without knowing what he is talking about."

Many other similar testimonies by men of world-wide reputation might be cited in support of the claims of Spiritualism. Survival after death is not a hope, a belief or a speculation. It is a scientifically proved fact. The accumulated evidence is beyond doubt ; no amount of criticism or denial can disprove it.   It is as stupid for a person who has not investigated the subject to say that it is untrue as it would be for a blind man to say that trees do not exist because he cannot see them.

I can only record what I myself have experienced. Others have recorded their experiences.   But all this evidence, contained in hundreds of books written on the subject, is but a minute fraction of what is daily being received, but never published. "To-day," says Dr. Hans Driesch, "the actuality of psychic phenomena is doubted only by the incorrigible dogmatist."   At that I must leave the evidence I have adduced in support of the truth of Spiritualism, and I do so in the hope that it may at least have awakened some interest in the vital question, "If a man die shall he live again?" In these days of bereavement and sorrow, endless misery is caused by people being in ignorance of the truth.   This subject is one which any one may investigate for himself.   And he who seeks with a fearless and open mind will surely find a rich reward.

Why should we weep? We do not bury love;
The dust of earth but claims its kindred dust.
We do not drop our jewels in the grave,
And have no need to seek our treasures there.

Gerald Massey.

CHAPTER XII.

THE RELIGIOUS ASPECT OF SPIRITUALISM.

A VISITOR to London, for the first time, would naturally want to spend part of his time seeing some of the sights of the capital of the Empire. He would want to see Buckingham Palace, Westminster Abbey, the Houses of Parliament, and I have no doubt he would include in his list the Tower of London.

Let us suppose that our friend leaves his hotel to visit the Tower. In due time he arrives at one of the massive gateways giving access to that historic pile of buildings. But if his journey ends there, if he stands looking at the gateway for a few moments and then retraces his steps to his hotel, he cannot say that he has seen much of the Tower itself. Even if he repeats this performance every day for a week and never gets any further than the gateway, he will still be unable to say that he knows much of the Tower of London. But if he passes through the gateway, crosses the courtyard and enters the building, he will see many interesting things. And among others he will no doubt be conducted to the Wakefield Tower, where he will be shown the Crown Jewels of England.

Now, this imaginary episode bears a close relation to the study of Spiritualism. There are many jewels in Spiritualism, but there are also many people who never see them, because they never get beyond the " gateway " of the seance room. I am not in any way disparaging the seance room. Very far from it. I know that in countless cases the seance room has been the means of convincing people that the claims of Spiritualism are true. But what I want to emphasise is that the seance room is not the end of Spiritualism, rather is it only the beginning. It is the gateway through which the great majority of people come into Spiritualism, but there is a great deal more in Spiritualism than the seance room can provide.

Spiritualism does not merely consist of knowing that life persists after the death of the physical body, and that communication with the so-called dead is an every-day occurrence in which all may take part. It goes a long way further than that. The fact of survival, as Spiritualists understand the meaning of the word, carries with it many implications concerning not only our future life but our present life as well. Spiritualism does not only deal with what we call the " next world," as some people wrongly imagine. It has a great deal to tell us about this world also. It does not confine its attention to those who have passed into the world of spirit. It has much to say to us about ourselves and our relation to this world of matter in which we are now living.

Most of us, through our early training, have been accustomed to look upon ourselves as physical beings who possess within us a mysterious something

which we call a " soul " ; although I imagine that
if anyone were to ask the average man in the street
what his soul really is, he would rarely obtain a
correct or satisfactory answer to his question.
But Spiritualism tells us that if we look upon
ourselves in that light we are wrong. We are,
so to speak, looking upon ourselves through the
wrong end of a telescope—the end which makes us
appear very much smaller than we really are.
Spiritualism tells us that, in reality, we are not
physical beings at all ; we are spiritual beings who
have been given the use of a physical body for such
time as we require it here on earth. It impresses
upon us that our existence cannot be bounded by
any such terms as Time or Space, but that life
continues, onward and upward, not only in this
world but in the realms of spirit as well, where
Time and Space no longer exist.

" This world is but the childhood of Eternity,"
said Charles Kingsley, and the teaching of
Spiritualism confirms that we must only look upon
it in that light. It is merely the elementary school-
room, in which we learn our childish lessons which
will be of use to us in the greater life beyond. In
fact, it is only when we have cast aside our earthly
body and have emerged into that greater life that
we are able to give full expression to our real and
true selves.

One of the best definitions of Spiritualism I
know is that it is " The Art of Spiritual Unfoldment," because in that definition we find the true
reason for our existence here on earth. We have

been placed in this world for that very purpose
—to unfold our spiritual nature, and the only way
in which we can do that is by developing that part
of us which we call our Character. The more we
set ourselves to do that; the harder we strive,
in this life, after what we know to be right and
good, the better are we fitting ourselves for the
greater life which lies before us.

But the phrase, " The Art of Spiritual Unfoldment," might also be used to define Religion, a
word which always has been, and still is, a much
abused and misused term. We speak of the
Christian religion, the Jewish religion, the
Mohammedan religion, the Hindoo and Buddhist
religions. We compare them one with the other,
in much the same way as we would compare the
opposing views of the candidates at a Parliamentary
election, as if they must necessarily be antagonistic
to each other. But what do these different
designations really imply? Do they not imply
that, all over the world throughout the centuries
of the past, various peoples have at different times
and in different ways been striving to express their
own ideas, and put into words their own thoughts,
regarding spiritual things? The word " religion "
is derived from the Latin *re*, again, and *ligo*, I bind.
It denotes that spiritual emotion or urge within
each individual which binds, or unites, us to some
Unseen Power whom we worship and to whom we are
willing to give our obedience. The object of religion
is to " bind us again " to that Power, by whatever
means we may use and by whatever name It may be
called.

It is a common fallacy among some people that religion consists of nothing more than belonging to some particular church or sect. To others it means joining some religious order and withdrawing themselves from the world to within the cloisters of a monastery or nunnery. Others again will say that religion depends on partaking regularly and frequently of certain sacraments and indulging in certain ritualistic ceremonies. While still others are content to call a person religious provided he attends more or less regularly at some place of worship and takes an active interest in church affairs.

Now, all these things may be very well in their way, but people may do any, or all, of them and still not know the true meaning of the word "religion." Religion does not consist in church-going or sacraments, in ritual or ceremonial. The people who indulged in that sort of thing nineteen hundred years ago were the very people whom Jesus condemned so strongly. He told them quite plainly that, in spite of all their religious observances, they were still far from the Kingdom of God. If religion is to be of any value at all it must mean a great deal more than that, and what may be of religious value to one person may be of little or no value to another.

I dare not say to my neighbour "your conception of religion is wrong because it differs from mine." He might equally well say the same about me. And a third person might join in the conversation and say the same about both of us. We are told that, physically, no two persons are exactly alike. Spiritually, the same distinction applies. Each individual has his, or her, own separate and personal need which that person alone knows, and which only that person's own particular conception of religion can supply. It is thus impossible to define religion in terms of any particular creed or any precise set of doctrines. Religion must spring from the heart, not from the head, and the object of our worship may be known by many different names just as it may be worshipped in many different ways. We in this western world call the Power whom we worship, God. Elsewhere, millions of devout souls who belong to the Mohammedan faith call it Allah. The Hindoo calls it Vishnu, while the North American Indian calls it simply The Great White Spirit. But all these names, and many others, indicate one and the same object—an undefinable " Something " or " Someone " whom we instinctively recognise as the source of our being and to whom we are prepared to give our allegience.

Religion, then, is part of our innermost spiritual nature and lies deep within each one of us. It is a natural craving of the mind just as food and drink are natural cravings of the body. Doubtless that is why it has so often been exploited by those who have preyed on the credulity of sincere but ignorant people throughout the centuries. In order to amass wealth and power for themselves they have exploited the emotional side of human nature by turning religion into systems of theological beliefs, and by holding before the people the fear of ultimate perdition if they did not believe what they chose to teach. In consequence of this, a welter of confused and contradictory teaching has come into existence, and the world to-day is divided into countless water-tight compartments of so-called religious thought, the votaries of each firmly believing not only that their particular belief is the only one containing the truth but that the followers of all others are eternally condemned.

And into the midst of all these varied and conflicting ideas and beliefs comes Spiritualism, which during the comparatively short space of less than a hundred years has spread throughout the world in a truly astonishing way. Its phraseology has even penetrated into our every day speech. We now frequently hear people speak of " passed on " instead of " died " ; the words " psychic," " trance," " clairvoyant," and so forth, have become ordinary terms of conversation. But its influence has extended far beyond that. No longer do we hear the " hell-fire " sermons of fifty years ago. The teaching of the orthodox churches to-day regarding death and the after-life is so entirely different from what it was half a century ago that it would shock our grandparents ! Officially, the doctrines of the churches remain unaltered, but on every side we hear the remark " Oh, but nobody believes that now ! " Spiritualism is steadily and remorselessly exposing the fallacy of many of the old theological dogmas, belief in which was once looked upon as being absolutely essential, and which constituted what people once called " religion " to the exclusion of everything else. It has destroyed the bogey that man is nothing better than a miserable sinner

and in its place has given the world a new gospel
—the gospel of man's inherent spiritual nature.
It teaches that, far from being born in sin and
under the wrath of God, we have been born with the
Divine spirit already within us.

Life is a journey which climbs onward and
upward.   Even now we may catch glimpses of the
life that is to be, a life which is ideal, a life in which
goodness, virtue and truth hold sway.   But instead
of realising that he has within him the power to
make that journey himself, man has turned religion
into a kind of hand-rail on which he may lean for
support, ignoring the fact that all the hand-rails
in the world cannot relieve anyone from the
responsibility of having to do the climbing himself.
Even if you hold on to a hand-rail going upstairs
it is you who must make the effort which gets you
to the top.   The hand-rail may help you but it
does not do the work.   Spiritualism teaches
Personal Responsibility.   It rejects the doctrine
that we can shift that responsibility on to anybody
else's shoulders, and asserts that the unfoldment
of our spiritual nature must depend on our individual
effort alone.   And it is that effort which we all have
to make in climbing the staircase of life which
develops our character, and makes us what we are
and what we shall be throughout eternity.

What was the secret of the life of Jesus—that
life which has been an inspiration to millions of
human beings, not only within the fold of the
Christian church but far beyond it, during the past
1900 years ?   Was it not that he knew he had that
power within him ; that he knew that, through all

the vicissitudes of life he could call on that power
to give him the strength he required? We are so
apt to forget that Jesus was just a human man
like ourselves; that he had to face temptations and
difficulties just as we do. If he had been immune
from all these obstacles in life which beset each one
of us, he would not have understood our human
frailties and his life would have been of no value
as an example for us to imitate. But it was just
because he demonstrated, in all the crises of his life,
that he did possess that power and that he could
call it to his aid, that he was able to show us the way
which we should follow.

So when the Spiritualist says that the purpose
of our lives is to develop our spiritual nature, he
means that the purpose of life should be to liberate
that Divine power which lies within us and which,
perhaps unconsciously, is continually urging us on to
higher and better things. And as we liberate that
power, so do we allow the God within to work in us
and through us, not only for our own personal good
but for the good of others and the advancement of
His cause. Thus we find, in Spiritualism, the
secret of that intimate union between God and man
—that " binding again " of the Divine within us
to the source of our Divinity—which we call
Religion, and which is the birthright of every
human soul.

Spiritualism, then, is not merely " a " religion,
it is—Religion. When we talk of " a " religion we
infer that there is more than one. We do not want
Spiritualism to become merely a religion. History

shows us only too clearly that in the past there has been more quarrelling and wrangling and bitterness caused by rivalry between different forms of religion than by anything else on earth. We must not allow Spiritualism to get mixed up in anything of that sort.   But we can truly call it RELIGION—plain and simple Religion. It reveals to us our personal relationship to the Universal Fatherhood of God and to the world-wide Brotherhood of Man.   And not only does it unite us to God and to our fellow-men on earth, it also unites us to those who have passed on to the unseen world beyond.   And by doing that—by bringing us into contact with those whom we have " loved long since and lost awhile "—it has once and for all destroyed that dreaded monster, the Fear of Death, which need never have existed but which has haunted the minds of men and women for centuries.

Spiritualism is the only means by which that fear can be dispelled.   Instead of giving us merely a vague faith it gives us definite knowledge. Through Spiritualism alone we learn something of the real nature of the Spirit World to which we are travelling, and of the life we shall live when we get there. Once that fear has been dispelled and man has come to realise that, even now, he is a spiritual being who cannot die, the " hand-rails " of religious creeds, rituals and ceremonials will be thrown away.   Along with them will go the multitude of sectarian labels to which so many people cling so desperately, as if they were the only passports which can possibly carry them into heaven. And in place of creeds and sects there will emerge the one and only religion the world had ever need to know of—the spiritual bond of love and brotherhood between man and man which was the very essence of the teaching of Jesus, and which unites each and every one to his fellows and to the Universal Father of All.

I have already said that the word "Religion" is a much abused term. Another word similarly abused is "Christian." Who is a Christian? The orthodox church claims that a Christian is one who is a member of one or other of its numerous denominations or sects and accepts its creeds and doctrines. The dictionary, on the other hand, defines a Christian as "a follower of Jesus Christ." Unfortunately, these two definitions are not always synonymous. A follower of Jesus need not be a member of any Christian church. Similarly, if judged by their conduct, many members of these churches are far from being followers of Jesus. As a nation the Germans are Christians. They have their Christian bishops, priests and pastors, as in any other Christian country. But nowhere do I find that Jesus taught that his followers were to indulge in the massacre and torture of those whose political opinions differ from their own. The ghastly history of the Concentration Camps, the deliberate murder and starvation of millions of innocent men, women and children, and the terrible disclosures of the foulest atrocities, systematically committed by the Germans in almost every country in Europe, all testify to the fact that 800 years of Christian creeds and doctrines, preached from thousands of pulpits throughout the land, have done nothing to raise the Nazi hordes above the savagery of the brute.

If a Christian is only " a member of the Christian church" the past six years have made it abundantly clear that to be called a Christian may be far from being a compliment.   In fact, if we go back ten years instead of six, we find another Christian nation, the Italians, whose country is actually the birthplace of Christianity and the headquarters of by far the largest sect in that religion, pursuing similar methods of savagery when subduing the people of Abyssinia, bombing innocent natives and throwing their prisoners-of-war out of aeroplanes, so as to terrorise the inhabitants into submission to a rule which they abhorred.   While the people of Spain, the most priest-ridden country in Europe and therefore, presumably the most Christian, have during the same period slaughtered each other like cattle in the course of a political civil war.   The same sorry tale can be told of so-called Christian countries throughout the past 1600 years, and to make matters worse the so-called Christian church has usually been at the bottom of the trouble.   What resemblance there may be between that sort of behaviour and the teachings of Jesus is hard to discover.

On the other hand, if we accept the dictionary definition of the word, that a Christian is " a follower of Jesus Christ," there is no reason on earth why a Spiritualist should not claim that title if he wishes to do so.   In fact, Spiritualists maintain that the teachings of Spiritualism, and the form of our devotional services, are in full accord with the practices of the early Christian churches in the 2nd and 3rd centuries. As will be seen as we proceed I make further reference to this point in a later chapter.

Meanwhile, we may here state the Seven Principles of Spiritualism, which are as follows :— We believe in

1.—The Fatherhood of God.
2.—The Brotherhood of Man.
3.—The Communion of Spirits and the Ministry of Angels.
4.—The continuous existence of the Human Soul.
5.—Personal Responsibility.
6.—Compensation and retribution hereafter for all good and evil deeds done on earth.
7.—Eternal progress open to every human soul.

Let us examine these Principles, and we shall find that without exception they are in no way incompatible with the teachings of Jesus of Nazareth.

1.—THE FATHERHOOD OF GOD.

This means the *universal* Fatherhood of God, not that He is merely the Father of those who hold certain religious beliefs. Spiritualists maintain that every member of the human race, either in this world or in the world beyond, is a child of God ; that He is the Father of All. God has no favourites. His love extends to the sinner as well as to the saint, whether the sinner still lives on this earth or has passed through the change called " death." No person has the right to dictate to a child how he must

13

approach his earthly father. The child must decide that for himself. Similarly, no person has the right to say how any human being must approach God.

Some years ago the Rev. Professor Cameron, Professor of Systematic Theology at the Free Church College in Edinburgh, complained that the new school catechism taught "the universal love of God." In this catechism, he said, all men alike were represented as being the objects of God's love and God was represented as being their Father. "Such teaching," said Professor Cameron, "would instil into the minds of the young the ruinous fiction of the Universal Fatherhood of God."

Now, it would be unfair to suggest that these are the views of the clergy as a whole. Although they would be the last to admit it, the influence of Spiritualism on clerical opinion during the past fifty years or so has been very marked. But the Rev. Professor Cameron is a man of considerable prominence in the assemblies of the church. At his jubilee the Moderator of the church referred to him as "a notable figure" and as one who had "played a valiant part" in the church's affairs. His words, then, especially in his capacity as a Professor of Theology, must have carried great weight among the faithful.

But is the voice of Theology the same as the voice of Jesus? Jesus taught "Our Father, which art in Heaven." He was not addressing Christians. These words were uttered 300 years before the Christian church, as we know it to-day, came into existence. He was speaking as a Jew, to his fellow-Jews and to any others who might happen to be listening to him. "Not every one that saith unto me, Lord, Lord, shall enter into the kingdom of heaven, but he that doeth the will of my Father which is in heaven." Spiritualists accept these words as applying to every member of the human race, irrespective of colour, country or creed. If these words are true the words of Professor Cameron are false. God is the Father of all mankind.

2.—THE BROTHERHOOD OF MAN.

If God is our Father we are all His children, and between us there must of necessity exist the family link of Brotherhood. The black man is the brother of the white man, just as the brown man is the brother of the yellow man. A Buddhist is the brother of a Christian, so is a Hindoo the brother of a Jew. A Chinaman is the brother of a Britisher. An Arab in the desert is the brother of an American multi-millionaire. This Principle is, or should be, the foundation of all human society. It was taught by Jesus, but like many of his teachings it has never been put into practice. Far from the human race being a family of brothers, selfishness, greed and personal or national ambition have made it a community of thieves and cut-throats. It is well said that history is the record of man's folly. It is certainly not the record of human brotherhood. Once the teaching of Jesus, as embodied in the 2nd Principle of Spiritualism, were put into effect, the face of the world would change as if touched by a magic wand. There would be no more war. Industrial conditions would be revolutionised. Poverty and much avoidable disease would be abolished, and the taxpayer would, among other things, be relieved of the necessity of feeding and clothing the inmates of our prisons. Such places would cease to exist. The duties of the police would be confined to waving their arms at cross-roads and blind corners! People would become honest and live honestly, and no Robert Burns of the future would ever need to write that " Man's inhumanity to man makes countless thousands mourn."

An impossible ideal, you may say! An ideal, yes, but not impossible. Jesus treated all men as his brothers. So did Gautama the Buddha, St. Francis of Assisi and other great and noble souls. Why should it be impossible for us to do the same ?

The next two Principles may be considered together. They are :—

3.—THE COMMUNION OF SPIRITS AND THE MINISTRY OF ANGELS.

4.—THE CONTINUOUS EXISTENCE OF THE HUMAN SOUL.

In view of what I have already written in this book I need not devote much space to either of these Principles. But as the object of my referring to them here, as a whole, is to show that the beliefs of Spiritualism are in no way antagonistic to the teachings of Jesus, one or two instances recorded in the gospels will suffice.

Jesus himself demonstrated the Communion of Spirits in the most practical way possible, namely, by appearing himself after his death not only to his disciples but, according to St. Paul, to " above five hundred brethren at once," and later to Paul himself on the road to Damascus. He further gave his sanction to this communion by speaking, on the Mount of Transfiguration, with Moses and Elias in the presence of three of his followers. He accepted the Ministry of Angels both after the Temptation in the Wilderness and in the Garden of Gathsemane, where " there appeared an angel strengthening him." There was nothing miraculous about any of these occurrences. Such incidents took place before the time of Jesus, just as they have taken place since. " He shall give his angels charge over thee," said the Psalmist. Jesus knew the truth of this 1900 years ago. Spiritualists know the truth of it to-day.

The fact that Jesus, Moses and Elias all appeared on earth after their death is, in itself, sufficient proof of the Continuous Existence of the Human Soul. It is the belief of all the great religions of the world. It has now been proved in these modern days by Spiritualism to be true. " The phenomena of Spiritualism," wrote Alfred Russell Wallace, F.R.S., " are proved quite as well as any facts are proved in other sciences." To faith has been added knowledge. Belief is now a certainty.

5.—PERSONAL RESPONSIBILITY.

It is on this Principle that there is a complete break between the teaching of Spiritualism and

that of the orthodox churches. The fundamental
faith of the Christian church is that man is a
sinner and can only be saved as the result of a
vicarious atonement. Any person who does not
believe this is eternally lost. It would be interesting
to know how many of the millions of people who
profess to believe this doctrine are aware that,
so far as the three oldest gospels are concerned,
only two short references to this vitally important
belief are reported to have been made by Jesus.
And both of them were made in private to his
disciples alone. So far as we know, during the
entire course of his public ministry, Jesus never
once made any remark which even suggested that
his death was to be in the nature of a sacrifice for
sin. If it really were to be so, it is incredible that
he did not make it the central theme of all his
preaching. Instead, he preached the exact opposite ;
he even quoted the words of the prophet Hosea,
" It is mercy that I desire, not sacrifice."

No ; the doctrine of atonement through the
death of a victim was not taught by Jesus, it was
introduced into the teaching of the early church
by Paul, the converted Jew, who, with no authority
but his over-vivid imagination, took upon himself
the responsibility of comparing the death of Jesus
with the Jewish sacrifice, about which we read so
much in the Old Testament. And on this flimsy
foundation the Christian church has built a colossal
edifice, from which it excludes all who accept the
teaching of Jesus and reject the teaching of Paul.
Spiritualists accept the teaching of Jesus. They

know that as a man sows so shall he reap. A
sinner may repent on his death-bed, but his
repentance does not " wash away " his sin and give
him a free and immediate passport into the presence
of God.

To carry the doctrine of the vicarious atonement
to its logical conclusion, if Hitler or any of his
fellow-criminals repent when they are on the brink
of death,* they will at once become " redeemed,"
and, in the words of the Westminster Confession
of Faith, " being then made perfect in holiness
(will be) received into the highest heavens, where
they (will) behold the face of God in light and
glory." Should such a fantastic transformation
scene take place, which no intelligent person can
believe for a moment, I imagine that the most
uncomfortable people in that august assembly
would be Hitler & Co. themselves ! To say that
they would feel entirely out of place in such company
is to put it mildly ! As for the millions of Jews
whom these men have been instrumental in
slaughtering by every ghastly means in their power,
can we believe that while their foul murderers are
enjoying the bliss of heaven because they have been
" saved " by a death-bed repentance, they, poor
souls, are to be writhing in hell, simply because they
are Jews ? Such a belief is blasphemy. God is
Love, and love and justice go hand-in-hand.

---

* This was written before Hitler's death in May, 1945.

This brings us naturally to the sixth Principle :—

6.—COMPENSATION AND RETRIBUTION HEREAFTER
    FOR ALL GOOD AND EVIL DEEDS DONE ON
    EARTH.

The sinner may repent, but he must work out
his own salvation. If he does not do so in this life
it must be done in the life to come. Death does not
put " paid " to any man's account with his Creator.
We must all experience the consequences of our
actions, irrespective of whether these have been
good or bad. Heaven and hell are not geographical
localities ; they are states of consciousness. The
only thing anyone has to fear when he crosses the
borderline of death is his conscience. The Prodigal
Son may have had " a good time " in the far
country, but by the time he turned for home he had
spent all his money. He had squandered his
father's " portion." In the years which followed,
while he was working and sweating to earn his living,
he must many a time have envied his brother who
had stayed at home, and who doubtless was living
a comfortable and easy life on the means which his
father eventually left him. But it was the
prodigal's own fault. He had been a fool, and
like all other fools he had to pay the price of his
folly. No one else could pay it for him. His
father did not punish him ; he punished himself.

When we reach the Spirit World we automatically
enter that state of spiritual consciousness for which
we have been fitting ourselves while we have been
on earth. We may find ourselves in the " seventh
heaven " of happiness or in the lowest hell of

remorse. The one will be our Compensation, the other our Retribution.

7.—ETERNAL PROGRESS OPEN TO EVERY HUMAN SOUL.

But the one in the hell of remorse is not condemned to remain there for eternity. His state is not one of finality. No earthly father would put his children into a room and say to them " You are to stay here for an hour. I shall watch you through the window, although you will not see me, and if you do anything which I think is wrong I shall punish you for the rest of your lives. I shall cast you out of my house, I shall disinherit you, I shall make your lives a constant misery." Why should we impute to God a course of conduct which, if indulged in by any earthly parent, would gain for him the opprobrium of every decent-minded individual and rightly land him either in a police cell or a lunatic asylum?

In my earlier book, " The Unbroken Melody of Life," I told the story of a man who had passed on after not being all he should have been in this life. Later, he came back and spoke to me. " I am beginning to see the light now," he said. He had realised the error of his ways and been ashamed; then he had set his foot on the ladder and begun to climb out of spiritual darkness. Now he was beginning to see the light, and the higher he climbs the stronger will the light become. Jesus taught that the love of God is such that, like a shepherd, he will leave the " ninety and nine " and go to seek for the one that is lost. His love for us does not end when we pass through the portals of death. He will still seek for the lost soul in the Great Beyond. And He will seek till He finds him. Those who in this war have received the dreaded news about some loved one who perhaps had caused them sorrow by his way of living, and regarding whose future after death they may be in agony of mind, need have no fear. The road of endless progression is open to *every* human soul, and even now his feet may be firmly planted on that road which eventually will lead him to the Kingdom of God. Thoughts of sympathy, love and forgiveness, and prayers for the help and guidance of angel ministers, will assist him on his upward journey.

These, then, are the Seven Principles on which Spiritualists base their beliefs. They maintain that they contain all of religion that man has need to know. If the teaching of Spiritualism is wrong, the teaching of Jesus was wrong. A Church of England clergyman once said to me, " If you ask my candid opinion, the best thing the church could do would be to put the Nicene Creed in the waste-paper basket and the Thirty-nine Articles in the fire, and then get back to the shores of the Sea of Galilee and humbly listen to the voice of the Master." He was right. But if the Church should take that clergyman's advice, which I must confess is extremely unlikely, and decide to embark on that journey, it will find that many people, including some whom it despises and considers lost, will have arrived there a long way before it.

CHAPTER XIII.

SPIRITUALISM AND THE LAW.

"AND now I say unto you, Refrain from these men and let them alone; for if this counsel or this work be of men, it will come to nought; but if it be of God, ye cannot overthrow it" (Acts 5, 38).

It will be remembered that this advice was given by Gamaliel, a doctor of the laws, to the priests of his day when they attempted to prevent the apostles from spreading abroad the teachings of Jesus. As I have already shown that these teachings were similar to those of Spiritualism to-day, it may well be said that the efforts of the Sanhedrin on that occasion were prompted by the same motives as have actuated the orthodox churches throughout the past sixteen centuries. The priests realised that this teaching was contrary to their personal interests and therefore, by fair means or foul, it must be suppressed.

The Sanhedrin, before which the apostles were arraigned, was the chief court of the nation, having particular jurisdiction over religious affairs. At the time of Jesus the Pharisaic party held the predominating influence in it, which accounts for its bitter antagonism towards the apostles and all who accepted the teaching of the Master. Fortunately, however, Gamaliel's advice was accepted by the members of that court and, as history has shown, he was right. The teachings of Jesus were "of God," and in spite of all the efforts of ecclesiastical and civil courts throughout the centuries they never have been, and never will be, overthrown.

But to turn from an incident which happened in Palestine nineteen hundred years ago to what takes place in Great Britain to-day, it is a tragic fact that if Jesus and certain of the apostles were now alive in this country, doing and saying the things recorded of them in the Bible, they would be regarded as criminals in the eyes of the Law and, as such, would be liable to arrest and punishment. The modern " Sanhedrin," or Courts of so-called Justice in this land, are not even so open-minded as their predecessor in Jerusalem ; the voices of our present-day Gamaliels fall on deaf ears. The Pharisees are still in control, and the attitude of the law towards Spiritualists suggests that it is the influence of this priestly class, and not the dictates of justice, which dominates the decisions of our judicial authorities.

But before we proceed further it would be well to define our terms, as many different words are in use to indicate communications with the Unseen. The Church, for example, calls it " the communion of saints," which phrase it defines as " a fellowship with the departed in prayer and worship " (Doctrine in the Church of England, p. 214). But a few lines further on we are informed " it is impossible to have well-grounded assurance that the saints hear us," consequently the alleged fellowship would not appear to be of much practical value. The Law, on the other hand, calls it by a variety of names, those chiefly used being " conjuration," " withcraft " and " vagrancy." Those who participate in this communication are known in legal phraseology as " rogues " and " vagabonds." Those who know something about the subject call it " Psychic Science " or " Spiritualism." So, to avoid confusion, the word Spiritualism will be used throughout this chapter to denote that personal contact with those in the Spirit World which every intelligent person to-day knows to exist.

The first Act of Parliament directed against Spiritualism was passed almost exactly 400 years ago, in the year 1541. Henry VIII. was on the throne, the statute known as The Six Articles, popularly called " the whip with six thongs," was in force, whereby orthodox religion of the strictest type was imposed on the people ; failure to believe in the doctrine of transubstantiation was punishable by death at the stake, and the country was being deluged in blood as the result of religious persecution. Froude, in his " History of England," draws a gruesome picture of conditions as they existed in those days of cruelty and tyranny. He writes :—

> " They went out into the highways and hedges ; they gathered up the lame, the halt and the blind ; they took the weaver from his loom, the carpenter from his workshop, the husbandman from his plough ; they laid hands on maidens and boys who had never heard of

any other religion than that which they were called on to abjure ; old men tottering into the grave and children whose lips could but just lisp the articles of their creed. And of these they made their burnt-offerings, with these they crowded their prisons, and when filth and famine killed them they flung them out to rot."

It was in this atmosphere of religious intolerance and bigotry that communication with the Spirit World, now known as Spiritualism, was first prohibited by law in this country.

A later Act was passed in the reign of James I. " for the better restraining of conjuration, enchantment and withcraft . . ." In his excellent pamphlet, " Psychic Science and Barbaric Legislation," Dr. Ellis T. Powell, LL.B., D.Sc., deals at some length with the extraordinary provisions of this Act. The Attorney General at that time was the notorious Sir Edward Coke, whom Dr. Powell describes as " the greatest lawyer of the age, who was also one of its foulest ruffians . . . (he) acted in defiance of justice, pity, remorse or even decency. Provided the Crown required the conviction of an innocent man, Coke was prepared to get it, no matter how foul the means he used." In those days any ignorant and unscrupulous scoundrel, who had the power to do so, could condemn a person to death with barely even the farce of a trial.

Coke's mentality can be judged by the fact that he defined a " conjurer " (one who conjures spirits), as " he that by the holy and powerful

name of Almighty God invokes and conjures the
Devil to consult with him or to do some act."
This was a felony and punishable by death.   In
these modern days of popular education and
scientific knowledge we might well laugh at this
ignorant and superstitious conception of spirit
intercourse, but for the fact, as we shall see, that
to " conjure spirits " is still regarded as an offence
against the law of this land.   Last year (1944)
a Spiritualist medium was sentenced to nine months'
imprisonment for this alleged offence.

Dr. Powell instances the case of a man named
Thomas Browne who, in the reign of Charles I.,
" wickedly, diabolically and feloniously made an
agreement with an evil and impious spirit."   It
is significant to note that this man's chief crime
was that, by entering into this so-called agreement,
he " promised and vowed to renounce the Lord and
Saviour Jesus Christ against the Catholic Christian
Faith, and to the grave scandal of the Christian
Religion and of all pious Christians, and to the
great displeasure of God Almighty."   The Christian
religion, apparently, entered as much into those
convictions of the ignorant and superstitious
17th century as it does into similar convictions
to-day.

The Act now on the Statute Book, under which
Spiritualist mediums are to-day prosecuted as
" conjurers," came into force in 1735, during the
reign of George II., a man of whose public and
private life the less said the better.   The state of
religious intolerance existing at that time was little,
if any, less brutal than that of the days of James I.

It is graphically described by the Rt. Hon. Thomas Johnston, P.C., M.P., in his "History of the Working Classes in Scotland," where, in reference to the burning of "witches"—now known as Mediums—he says :—

> "Interrogation before the Session, upon "evidence" elicited from poor distracted and hysterical victims by savage tortures, unknown even in the hellish annals of African heathendom, verdicts of guilty and sentences of roasting alive were pronounced ; and for a century and a half every Burgh and Parish in Scotland seems to have offered to heaven its regular incense of burning flesh."

He adds that when eventually Parliament no longer allowed old women to be burned alive at the sole discretion of the parish minister, " the only protests came from the clergy ! "

The Witchcraft Act of 1735, still in force, provides *inter alia* that " For the more effectual preventing and punishing of any Pretences to such Arts or Powers . . . whereby ignorant persons are frequently deluded and defrauded ; be it further enacted by the Authority aforesaid, That if any Person shall . . . pretend to exercise or use any kind of Witchcraft, Sorcery, Inchantment, or Conjuration, or undertake to tell Fortunes, or pretend, from his or her Skill or Knowledge in any occult or crafty science, to discover where or in what Manner any Goods or Chattels, supposed to have been stolen, or lost, may be found, every Person so offending . . . shall, for every such offence, suffer Imprisonment by the Space of one Whole Year."

This legally phrased clause can be summarised clearly in a few words. The person concerned must :—

  (1) Pretend to exercise some kind of witchcraft, sorcery, inchantment or conjuration ; or undertake to tell fortunes.

  (2) As a result of his, or her, skill or knowledge pretend to be able to say where lost or stolen goods can be found.

For these offences certain punishments are prescribed.

It will be noted that both of these charges include the word " pretend." It is the " pretending " to be able to do these things which constitutes the offence. Consequently, as this is the most important word in the clause, upon which guilt or innocence must be judged, it is of vital importance that the true meaning of the word is made clear. Any dubiety on that point at once renders the wording of the clause ambiguous and obscure.

What, then, is the meaning of the word " pretend " ?

Two standard dictionaries which I have consulted define the word " pretend " as—to assume ; to simulate ; to assert ; to claim ; to allege falsely. In modern English these various definitions do not all mean the same thing. For example, " to simulate " means " to imitate ; to mimic." But a person who " alleges falsely " does not either imitate or mimic. And one who " claims "

14

does not necessarily " allege falsely." He may consider that he has every right to the claim he makes.

The best example of this is one which is well known to everybody. It concerns an outstanding incident in the history of this country, about which there is no dispute and can therefore be cited as reliable evidence.

James Francis Edward Stuart was the son of James II. After the death of his father he was accepted by the party in this country known as the Jacobites as King of England. He " claimed " the throne of England under the style of James III. He is known as " The Old Pretender." His son, Charles Edward Stuart, made a similar claim. His landing from France in the Hebrides and his subsequent activities until his defeat at Culloden are too well known to need repetition here. " Bonny Prince Charlie " is known as " The Young Pretender."

The point I want to make is that neither of these men " alleged falsely," " assumed " or " simulated." They both made the definite *claim* to be the rightful King of England, and they are known as the " Pretenders," *because they made that claim*.

To give another example. As recently as last century a number of persons were charged in court with assaulting a woman " under the pretence of her being a witch." Here again the word " pretence " means " claim." The persons concerned *claimed* that the woman was a witch.

These examples, then, show that in the Witchcraft Act, which was placed on the Statute Book at the very time during which the claim by the Stuarts was being made, the word " pretend " means " to claim." That this is still the correct meaning of the word, in the legal sense, is shown by the fact that the law has power to charge a person with " obtaining money under false pretences "—in other words, by making a false claim.

It is worth noting that a further condition has to be complied with under the terms of the Witchcraft Act, namely, that the pretence must arise " from his or her skill or knowledge." Obviously, without the necessary skill or knowledge the accused person could not have made the claim. If he did not possess one or both of these qualifications his claim would not be a pretence ; it would be a " false " pretence. But the word " false " is not even mentioned in the Witchcraft Act, from one end of it to the other. Fraud, therefore, or even a suggestion of fraud, does not arise and consequently does not need to be proved before the accused is found guilty. So far as Spiritualists are concerned the bare fact that a person calls himself, or herself, a medium is in itself a crime. The genuineness or otherwise of the phenomenon produced through the medium does not fall to be considered. Genuineness is no defence ; it merely proves the medium's guilt.

Two legal decisions, both given in comparatively recent times, may be cited in support of this statement. The first occurred in 1877 when, in the case of Monck v. Hilton, Baron Pollock stated, when giving judgment, " dealing with the supernatural is in itself an offence." The other decision was given in 1904, when an indictment against palmistry was being tried. Here the judge stated " the question whether there is such a thing as palmistry or not is not the question at all here." The very fact that the accused had indulged in palmistry was, in itself, an offence, and the judge therefore refused to accept the evidence of expert palmists.

In the year 1824 another Act was passed, under which Spiritualists are to-day also prosecuted and punished. This was the Vagrancy Act, brought into force " for the punishment of idle and disorderly Persons, and Rogues and Vagabonds." This Act did not supersede the Witchcraft Act which, let me repeat, is still enforced against Spiritualists; it merely supplemented it by widening its scope. Among those chargeable under the Vagrancy Act are " every person pretending or professing to tell fortunes, or using any subtle craft, means, or device, by palmistry or otherwise, to deceive and impose on any of His Majesty's subjects." This, according to the law of this land, includes all Spiritualist mediums.

The short quotation I have just given from the Vagrancy Act forms part of a lengthy clause setting forth the various types of person against whom the Act is directed. Spiritualist mediums are thus herded together with (1) A woman deserting her bastard child; (2) A person in a public place exposing indecent prints or exhibitions; (3) A person lewdly and obscenely in a public place exposing his person with intent to insult a female;

(4) A male person who lives on the proceeds of prostitution or in a public place importunes for immoral purposes.

Our legal authorities carefully ignore the fact that both this Act and the Witchcraft Act of 1735 were placed on the Statute Book long before Modern Spiritualism came into existence. Nevertheless, our mediums, who include among them many well-known men and women who possess the psychic gift, are branded with the above-mentioned scum of the human family as " rogues and vagabonds," and are liable to be sentenced to three months' hard labour for no other crime than that they do possess that gift. The right of trial by jury is not allowed. Further, it is laid down in this Act that " it shall be lawful for any person whatsoever to apprehend any person who shall be found offending against this Act, and forthwith to take and convey him or her before some Justice of the Peace." If the alleged offender is handed over to a police officer who " shall refuse or wilfully neglect to take such offender into custody " the said police officer is to be fined a sum not exceeding five pounds.

On the second offence against this Act the " rogue " or " vagabond " becomes an " incorrigible rogue," which makes him, or her, liable to imprisonment for one year.

It is of interest to note that, in this Act, one of the punishable offences is that of endeavouring to procure charitable contributions " under any false or fraudulent pretence." Here we have the word " pretence " again used in its legal sense, namely, a " claim." But the person charged under the

same clause of the Act with telling fortunes—
in other words, the Spiritualist medium—is *not*
charged with committing this offence under any
"false or fraudulent pretence." In this case
fraud does not enter into the charge. Once again,
it is the *claim* itself which is the offence.

I have stressed this point so as to make it clear
that a Spiritualist medium does not require to
commit any offence before being arrested, prosecuted,
fined or imprisoned. The very fact that a person
is a medium makes him, or her, a criminal in the
eyes of the law. Lady Conan Doyle, for example,
if the police had chosen to take action against her,
would not have been able to say a single word in
her defence, even although she had engaged the
most eminent K.Cs. in the country to plead her case.
That very charming lady possessed the psychic gift
and practised it regularly in her home. Another
"criminal" was Air Chief Marshal Sir Trafford
Leigh-Mallory who, however, was considered a
sufficiently reputable individual to be General
Eisenhower's second-in-command when the Allies
landed in Normandy in 1944. Sir Edward Marshall
Hall, the famous K.C., confessed that he frequently
received messages from the Spirit World when in
court.

In the eyes of the law all of these well-known
persons were classed among the riff-raff of humanity,
solely because they possessed psychic powers which
they had probably inherited at birth, the psychic
strain being in many cases an hereditary gift, and
had they ever been brought into court they would
have been treated accordingly. And what applies

to them applies also to others of equally upright and honourable character, including, if reports be true, Mr. Winston Churchill, who has confessed to receiving writing through the planchette. This, in itself, is an offence, as it is one of the recognised methods by which people " pretend to hold communication with spirits "—a phrase recently added to the Vagrancy Act by our legal authorities (not with the consent of Parliament), so as to make certain of incriminating Spiritualists.

It may be asked what steps have Spiritualists taken to have the law amended so that these glaring disabilities, under which they suffer, may be removed ? Surely if the position were pointed out to the appropriate authorities the position would immediately be rectified and Spiritualists given the full measure of religious freedom enjoyed by other people.

The answer to that question is that Spiritualists have done everything in their power to have these laws amended, but have either been refused or have failed through being made the victims of political trickery.

In 1930 a deputation of prominent Spiritualists was received by Mr. J. R. Clynes, who at that time was Home Secretary, and in no uncertain terms they laid their case before him. I take the following short extracts from the speeches of some members of this deputation from Mr. Maurice Barbanell's booklet, " Rogues and Vagabonds," which gives a concise word-picture of the position of Spiritualists to-day under the laws now in force. Speaking of mediums, Sir Arthur Conan Doyle said

" These people . . . are living always under the shadow of the police. I would ask you to consider the administrative way in which the police act in these matters. They send to the medium disguised policemen and policewomen who pretend to be in trouble and ask for consolation, and then they take out a summons against the medium. That is being an *agent provocateur*, and the act, like the word, is not English; it is against all our feelings and traditions."

Mr. Ernest Oaten, editor of " The Two Worlds " and one of the best informed Spiritualists in this country, drove this point home by saying " We have reason to believe that in some cases *agents provocateur* have visited mediums ten or a dozen times, and failing to find evidence in his ordinary practice have deliberately put leading questions to such mediums for the purpose of extorting replies to questions and other information which would bring them within the law. This in practice is a distinct incitement to break the law." Mr. Oaten pointed out that Spiritualists have not been allowed to receive legacies left for the purpose of training mediums, on the grounds that mediumship is illegal ; also that the Charity Commissioners had refused to recognise a Spiritualist organisation which had been in existence for over 30 years, because the training of mediums was one of the objects stated in its Trust Deed. Cases had even arisen in which the right of Spiritualists to be interred in a church-yard had been disputed !

Mr. Hannan Swaffer, speaking as " an ordinary man of the world, who finds himself impelled to join the Spiritualist movement," said " People to-day are demanding proof of things which formerly they were content to believe. I could be of great service to people in this troubled age but for the fact that owing to a stupid and ridiculous and old-fashioned law, mediumship, which we consider sacred, is still illegal."

In his reply Mr. Clynes said that he had listened with " the deepest sympathy " to what had been said. He added, " As to the evidence of grievance under which you are labouring you have left me in no doubt." Turning to the more practical aspect of the question, he suggested that a private Bill should be introduced into Parliament, and he assured the deputation on behalf of the Government that *no difficulty would be placed in the way of having the case fully ventilated in the House of Commons.* So far as the official attitude of the Home Office was concerned, he stated " *The sole function of the Government in this matter is to protect the public against fraud, imposture and mental terrorism.*" I ask the reader to take particular note of these two sentences in italics. We shall see how much value can be placed on such assurances given by a member of His Majesty's Government.

The private Bill was duly prepared and was introduced into the House of Commons. It passed its first reading. Then something happened behind the scenes. The day of the second reading came round and, despite Mr. Clynes's assurance that the matter would be left to the free vote of the House, the Government Whips were placed at the door of

the Chamber, who advised members not to enter
while the debate was in progress. The result of
this action which can only be described as a piece
of political trickery was that, owing to there not
being a sufficient number of members in the House,
the Bill was " counted out." So much for the
Government's assurance that " no difficulty would
be placed in the way of having the case fully
ventilated in the House of Commons ! "

Mr. Clynes's further assurance that " the sole
function of the Government in this matter is to
protect the public against fraud, imposture, and
mental terrorism " has also proved to be a
worthless waste of words. In two cases, with
which I shall deal shortly at greater length,
Spiritualist meetings have recently been banned
on the grounds that such meetings were a
contravention of the Witchcraft Act. The question
of fraud or imposture did not arise, as the meetings
had not been held. The very fact that they
were to be held was, in itself, considered a sufficient
reason to arouse action on the part of the police.
There was to be nothing unusual about these
meetings ; they were to have been the ordinary
type of Spiritualist meeting which takes place in
any Spiritualist church or public hall any day of
the week. Nobody's mind was to be terrorised.
No threat of eternal damnation or hell fire was
to be held over the heads of those present if they
did not believe what was told them from the
platform. Mental terrorism is no part of the
teaching of Spiritualism, whatever part it may
play in that of other churches.

And yet these meetings were not allowed to take place. Those responsible for them were told that if they held them they would be breaking the law. So, apparently, the " sole function " of those in authority is not only to " protect the public " but by threat of punishment to prevent those who hold certain religious beliefs (which do not happen to meet with the approval of the orthodox hierarchy) from putting their beliefs into practice and worshipping God in the way which they honestly consider to be right.

Another deputation of Spiritualists visited the Home Office in July, 1943, but this met with no greater measure of success than the previous one in 1930. On this occasion Mr. Herbert Morrison, the Home Secretary, did not make the mistake of his predecessor, Mr. Clynes, in assuring Spiritualists of the Government's sympathy and consideration. Possibly he knew the secret of what had taken place behind the scenes before the second reading of the Bill which was so conveniently " counted out." Instead, he adopted a more subtle attitude. In a letter to Dr. Sydney J. Peters, M.P., announcing his decision in the matter, he stated :—

" I understand that it is the practice in some police forces in cases of this kind to institute proceedings only against persons whose activities have been the subject of complaint by members of the public and where there is evidence that the person is an impostor and taking money or other valuable consideration. Although I have no power to issue any directions

to the police as to the manner in which they
enforce the law, I have asked Chief Constables
to consider the adoption of this practice in
their forces. Further than this I cannot go,
but, if the practice I have described is generally
adopted persons bona fide engaged in the
ministrations of the Spiritualist churches and
in Psychical research should not find themselves
hampered by the provisions of the law."

On the surface this sounds a reasonable statement,
but it is not by any means so harmless as it appears.
If the legal advisers to the Home Office had done
their duty properly, Mr. Morrison must have known
of Baron Pollock's judgment that " Dealing with
the supernatural is in itself an offence, apart from
any deceiving or imposing on others." He must
therefore have known that, to Spiritualists, his
assurance was worthless. In fact he was bluntly
told in a letter written to him by Mr. J. B. McIndoe,
chairman of the Parliamentary Committee of the
Spiritualists' National Union, that it " savoured
almost of insult."

Mr. Morrison must have been fully aware that,
as the law stands to-day, *any* medium can be charged
with being an " impostor." He must have known
that the adoption by the police of the practice stated
was equivalent to giving them full authority to
discriminate between one " impostor " and another.
In other words, the police are to be the sole judge
as to which " impostor " is to be punished
and which is to be allowed to go free. Any person
who happens to have a quarrel with an individual

who practises the psychic gift has only to inform the
police that that individual is a medium who has
been " telling fortunes " or " conjuring spirits."
The police must then take action and, as mediumship
in itself is illegal, no defence against the charge
stands a chance of obtaining an acquittal.   As I
have already pointed out, " genuineness is no
defence."

On the other hand, mediums who may be used
by the Criminal Investigation Department in the
detection of crime, or society " clairvoyants " who
are patronised by the élite of the west end of London,
all of whom are equally " impostors " according
to the law, may, at the discretion of the police, be
allowed to remain at large.   If Mr. Morrison's
directions to the police force of this country are
allowed to stand we may well apply to our blue-
coated guardians of the law the words " Who made
thee a ruler and a judge over us ? "   It is no part
of the duties of the police to decide which law-
breaker will be punished and which will go scot-free.
Their duty is to bring *all* such before the bar of
justice (?) without fear or favour.

The public do not lodge complaints against
mediums with the police.   Such complaints are
invariably lodged by that unpleasant type of
individual known as the " common informer " who,
like the *agent provocateur*, is usually the tool of the
police.   I have never heard of a single case in which
a genuine sitter has laid any complaint against a
medium before the police, but I do know of several
cases where police officials have had sittings with
mediums and strongly object to the odious duty of

arresting such people, which they are frequently called upon to carry out.

In plain English, Mr. Herbert Morrison's letter simply means that he was not prepared to put a stop to the practice, already in vogue, of arresting mediums indiscriminately simply because they are mediums, and he must have known that the continuance of this practice, far from leaving Spiritualists " unhampered by the provisions of the law," left them precisely where they were before.   Events have since shown that this was the case.

That Mr. Morrison was not acting honestly in his dealings on this question is clearly demonstrated, firstly, by the fact that he refused the reasonable request that a committee should be appointed to inquire into the matter, and, secondly, by his ignoring a simple alternative by which the needs of justice would have been met.   If a medium is genuinely suspected of fraudulent conduct, or of being an impostor, the requirements of the law would be complied with by the simple procedure of charging that person with " obtaining money under false pretences."   Any lawyer will agree that this simple charge would meet the case.   Then why did he not advise Chief Constables to adopt this practice ? One can only form a conjecture, but possibly his reason was that, had he done so, the police authorities would have been placed in the position of having to *prove* that fraud had been committed, whereas, under the system at present in force, which he refuses to alter, fraud does *not* need to be proved before a conviction is obtained.

Lord Macauley once described certain trials which took place during the reign of Henry VIII. as " murder preceded by mummery." The methods adopted to-day for the suppression of Spiritualism may well be labelled " conviction preceded by cant."

Let us now turn our attention to the Law in action.

CHAPTER XIV.

THE LAW IN ACTION.

WHEN anyone is suspected of having committed a crime the police inquire into the matter, evidence of what has taken place is obtained, and when they are satisfied that the person is guilty a warrant is taken out for his arrest. Should the alleged crime have been brought to the notice of the police by a member of the public, a statement of his allegations is written down and the suspected person is given an opportunity of answering the charge. In the case of Spiritualist mediums, however, these rules do not apply. The ordinary methods of justice which, in this country at least, regard a person as being innocent until he is proved guilty, are dispensed with.

Where mediums are concerned the police methods are simple and direct. Usually what happens is this.

The attention of the police is drawn to the fact that Mrs. X. is a Spiritualist medium. This information is probably supplied by a "common informer," one of that detestable type of individual who sneaks in at the back door of a police office and "lays an information" against one of his fellow citizens. He knows that, in doing this, he runs no risk himself, as his name is not made public, and no matter what he may say about Mrs.

X. he is safe from any action being taken against him by her. After all, is he not acting as a loyal citizen under the terms of the Vagrancy Act, which lays upon him the duty of reporting such rogues and vagabonds to the custodians of the law?

The police then prepare for the pantomime that is to follow. There is really no need for them to go through this farce. If they chose to look in the local newspaper they would probably see there that Mrs. X. is advertised to give a demonstration of clairvoyance at some Spiritualist church the following Sunday. That, in itself, would convict her of being a medium and would render her liable to arrest. But the police elect to act otherwise. They find two persons—usually police women or policemen's wives—whom they dress up in mourning. One of them is given a wedding ring (if she happens to be a spinster) and is instructed to pass herself off as a widow whose husband has recently died. The other plays the part of her daughter or a friend, her real role, of course, being to corroborate what her colleague says when the case eventually comes into court.

These two women then proceed to Mrs. X's house and ask her if she will give them a " sitting." If questioned, they will glibly say that they sometimes attend the service in some Spiritualist church in the neighbourhood, that they have heard Mrs. X. give a demonstration of clairvoyance there, or make some other plausible excuse which disarms suspicion. After the sitting is over they return to police headquarters and concoct their story.

It really does not matter what they say. They can safely accuse Mrs. X. of having said or done anything they choose, as they know that when the medium comes up for trial it will be the word of two witnesses against one, and, in any case, Mrs. X. was probably in trance throughout the sitting and was therefore oblivious to everything that happened at the time. Usually a fee is paid, but that is not necessary to ensure conviction. Some mediums are under the impression that if they do not accept a fee they are immune from prosecution. That is not the case. A sitting given free is as much a crime as one for which payment is made.

Before long the medium receives a summons to appear in court. The two women impersonators go into the witness box and tell their story. All this, however, is a mere formality. The accused is a medium. She has given a sitting in that capacity. She is therefore found guilty and is either fined or sent to prison. It is a case of " heads I win ; tails you lose."

Some years ago a medium in the South of England told me how one day she had been going about her housework as usual when a ring came on the front-door bell. Two women were standing on the door-step. Would Mrs. ——— please give them a sitting ? The medium asked one or two questions, as a result of which her suspicions were aroused, so she told her visitors that she would give a sitting to one of them but not to both. They argued the point, saying that they wanted to sit together, but the medium remained firm in her decision and eventually, as the women evidently felt that they had gone too far to draw back, they agreed to this arrangement. One of them remained in one room while the other had a sitting in another. When it was ended she offered the medium a fee, but this was refused. As they were leaving the house the woman who had had the sitting suddenly " remembered " that she had left her umbrella in the room. She returned for it and both then took their departure.

Shortly afterwards the medium had occasion to go into the room where the sitting had been held, and lying on the mantelshelf she found a half-crown. She knew it had not been there before the sitting, so her suspicions became a certainty. Immediately she went to the police office, laid the half-crown on the counter and smilingly informed the officer in charge that " one of the ladies who called on me this morning must have left this by mistake ! " Needless to say the matter ended there !

But all mediums are not so fortunate as that. About three years ago a well-known London medium was the victim of a particularly outrageous prosecution, a garbled version of which appeared in the newspapers at the time. In this case the medium was the late Mrs. Stella Hughes, a lady whose husband takes a prominent part in public affairs in North London, and who, herself, was not only a popular figure among a large circle of friends, which included a number of well-known people, but was also one of the most gifted mediums in the country.

The usual police methods were adopted. Acting on information received from a " common informer "

two policewomen—Jean Stratton and Margaret Low
—discarded their uniforms, dressed themselves in
everyday clothes and called at Mrs. Hughes's
house. Stratton was a spinster, but she wore a
wedding ring so that Mrs. Hughes might be misled
into thinking that she was a married woman.
They told Mrs. Hughes that they had been
recommended to come to her by a friend, and by
representing that they were in deep distress through
bereavement they persuaded her to give them a
sitting.

Mrs. Hughes thought no more of the matter
until she received a summons to appear at
Marylebone Police Court to answer a charge under
the Vagrancy Act for fortune telling. The only
two witnesses for the prosecution were the two
women, Stratton and Low, and I was told afterwards
that their evidence was far from being convincing.
They " shuffled and mumbled " during examination
and made contradictory statements one would
imagine should have convinced any magistrate
that their story was not genuine. For example,
one of them stated that she had been keeping a
watch on Mrs. Hughes's house for some time, but
later, when asked why she had been late for an
appointment there, she replied that she " didn't
know the way to it." However, the magistrate
accepted this conflicting evidence in preference to
that of Mrs. Hughes, who emphatically denied the
statements which both witnesses had made against
her. She was convicted and fined £10 and costs,
and her name was added to the " black list " of
rogues and vagabonds which includes the dregs of

humanity, such as I have enumerated in the previous chapter.

As Mrs. Hughes was a well-known woman the case was reported at some length in the newspapers. But the connection between her conviction and what followed, if it ever came near the printing-press, was carefully censored and not made public.

A few months later the same two women, on whose evidence alone Mrs. Hughes had been convicted, were themselves arrested and found guilty in the same court of systematic theft. It was part of their duties, as policewomen, to keep watch over certain houses in the district whose occupants were from home, and this trust they had abused to such an extent that they had feloniously entered these houses and between them had stolen something like 500 articles of value. Obviously this criminal activity had been going on over a considerable period of time. It is almost certain that they must have been engaged in it at the date on which they had given evidence against Mrs. Hughes. When accused, one of them stated that certain of the articles found in her possession belonged to her landlady. Later, however, she confessed that she had been lying and that they formed part of the stolen property. Both women were dismissed from the police service and were sentenced to twelve months' imprisonment. But the fact that they were the same two women who had deliberately been used by the police to trick Mrs. Hughes into committing a " crime " and had given evidence against her was carefully suppressed.

Mr. Hannan Swaffer, who had taken a personal interest in the case, immediately wrote to Mr. Herbert Morrison, the Home Secretary at that time, appealing to him that, in view of these disclosures which exposed the type of women Stratton and Low were, Mrs. Hughes should be granted a King's Pardon.

Now, Mr. Swaffer and Mr. Morrison are old friends. They belong to the same political party and Mr. Swaffer has frequently spoken in support of Mr. Morrison's candidature at elections. I cannot therefore believe that Mr. Morrison would have refused Mr. Swaffer's appeal if he had been a free agent and felt himself able to comply with his request. But refuse it he did. The appeal was made solely on the grounds that the Vagrancy Act lays down that conviction must be obtained as the result of evidence given by " credible " witnesses, and no sane person could possibly term as " credible " two witnesses who had admitted and been convicted of both falsehood and theft. I have read Mr. Morrison's reply to Mr. Swaffer's letter. It evades the issue altogether, and is so short and pointless that it is obvious the writer was ill at ease on the subject and wanted to dispose of it in as few words as possible.

There was a " hidden hand " behind Mr. Morrison's refusal, just as there was a " hidden hand " behind the political trickery which prevented Spiritualists getting their Bill through its second reading in the House of Commons twelve years before, and just as there is a " hidden hand " behind every attempt so persistently made to destroy Spiritualism by bringing its followers into disgrace and disrepute. Only when the public become sufficiently educated in the facts of psychic science, and able to appreciate the vital truths embodied in the teachings of Spiritualism, will that " hidden hand " be forced through the pressure of public opinion to desist from its underground intrigues and leave our mediums unmolested.

But I cannot end this account of Mrs. Hughes's conviction without adding by way of postscript a short paragraph from Mr. Barbanell's booklet, " Rogues and Vagabonds," which requires no comment as it speaks for itself. He writes :—

" Just before these two policewomen were convicted the Spiritualist movement was startled by the possibility of a new kind of menace. Gladys Spearman, a medium well-known in London, was giving a sitting to two women on the premises of the Balham Spiritualist Society. After the sitting the women revealed that they were police officers. A detective later told the medium that she would be charged under the Vagrancy Act. Had this case come to court it would have been the first in which a medium would have been prosecuted as a result of a seance given on church premises. But the case never came to court. The two women were Stratton and Low, and after they had visited Gladys Spearman they had been sent to prison."

Evidently Mr. Herbert Morrison, or his advisers, and Scotland Yard differ in their opinions as to what constitutes a "credible" witness. Mr. Morrison considers that two persons convicted of falsehood and theft do come under that category. The police wisely thought otherwise and decided that a criminal's cell was a more appropriate place for them than the witness box. So Mrs. Spearman heard no more about it !

But recently the net has been spread more widely. Mrs. Hughes and Mrs. Spearman had at least committed an act which the law maintains is illegal. One was punished, the other was not. But a few months ago a new form of persecution was introduced.

It is all very well for the Home Secretary to write to Dr. Sydney Peters, M.P., telling him that the practice of the police is to institute proceedings only against persons who are "impostors," and that all others will be unmolested. He made a similar statement in the House of Commons which was published in the daily press and no doubt many people believed it was true. But what are the actual facts of the case?

Within the past few months two incidents have occurred in which the police have not only made no attempt to prove that the persons concerned were impostors; they have attacked the churches for which these persons were working. They have taken steps which prevented these churches from holding Spiritualist meetings. They have issued warnings that, if such meetings were held, those responsible for them would be in danger of prosecution under the Witchcraft Act.

The first of these incidents occurred at Altrincham, Cheshire, where the members of the local Spiritualist church had arranged for a lecture to be given by a prominent Spiritualist, Mr. W. H. Lilley, of London. Mr. Lilley is a healing medium. Much might be written regarding his work in that important field of Spiritualism which has no bearing on the incident I am relating, but it is necessary for me to record that Mr. Lilley is controlled by a spirit doctor named Dr. Letari, and that, while in a state of trance, Dr. Letari speaks through him with great fluency on subjects pertaining to bodily health and healing by spiritual means. The names of Mr. Lilley and Dr. Letari are well known among Spiritualists throughout the country, with the result that when one of these lectures is to be delivered the demand for accommodation generally exceeds that which the average church can provide.

Such was the case at Altrincham, and in order to accommodate as many people as possible the officials of the church there engaged the Town Hall for the meeting. Posters were printed and displayed, among other places, at the local railway station. Arrangements had been completed, when suddenly the police intervened. They informed the civic authorities that if the meeting was held in the Town Hall they, the authorities, would be liable to prosecution. They would be aiding and abetting a breach of the law. At the same time representations were made to the railway company who were told that they were equally guilty in displaying posters advertising the meeting.

These warnings had the desired effect. The civic authorities cancelled the let of the hall and the posters at the railway station were removed. As no other hall was obtainable the members of the Spiritualist church were forced to hold the meeting elsewhere, beyond the jurisdiction of the Altrincham police, where presumably the " hidden hand " did not wield the same degree of power.

The other incident occurred at Redhill, Surrey, where the police notified the president of the local Spiritualist church that if any further Spiritualist services were held in the building it would be closed, such services being a violation of the Witchcraft Act. When the president asked the police what activities had taken place in the church to warrant their interference, the only reply given was the evasive statement, " It is not what you have done but what you might do." The police officer who made this astonishing statement went on to say that, under the Witchcraft Act, all forms of mediumship were illegal, and that consequently it would be his duty to arrest and prosecute any mediums conducting a service of that nature in the church. He ended by forcing the president to sign an undertaking that all demonstrations of mediumship in the church would immediately be discontinued, threatening that if this were not done prosecution would follow.

In view of this persistent persecution which is systematically being directed against Spiritualist churches and societies, for the express purpose of destroying mediumship and bringing Spiritualism into disrepute, what value can be placed on statements such as those made by the Home Secretary which I have already quoted? Chief Constables openly ignore his advice. They laugh at his timid requests that they should not interfere with what he calls "bona fide" Spiritualists, and they do so because they know that he is powerless to prevent them taking whatever action they please, so long as this obsolete two-hundred-year-old Act remains on the Statute Book. Why should an Act which, if the Home Secretary is right, only applies to "impostors" be used to prevent services being held in any Spiritualist church, by unspecified mediums who might visit that church at any future date? The answer is simple. All mediums are "impostors," according to the law of the land, and if the Home Secretary is not aware of that fact he must be very badly advised.

In a recent prosecution Sir Gerald Dodson, Recorder of the City of London, stated "Spiritualists are only responsible to the law when fraudulent practices are proved." This statement has been shown over and over again to be untrue. What fraudulent practices were proved at Altrincham and Redhill, where meetings were banned before they ever took place? In the case I have mentioned, during the course of which Sir Gerald Dodson made this extraordinary remark—which, as a lawyer, he must have known was not in accordance with the wording of either the Witchcraft or the Vagrancy Acts—the medium offered to prove her genuineness by giving a demonstration of her mediumistic powers. Her offer was refused. But, even if she had succeeded in convincing everybody in court that she was genuine, that would have made no difference to the outcome of the case. The accused was a medium. She admitted that she was a medium. Therefore she was guilty. The legal decision of Baron Pollock still stands unaltered, " dealing with the supernatural is itself an offence, apart from any deceiving or imposing on others." The action of the police at Altrincham, Redhill, and elsewhere confirms this to be the case.

The function of the Government, said Mr. Clynes, is to protect the public from mental terrorism, but these incidents show that it does not hestitate to use that weapon, itself, when it suits its purpose to do so. If the Government would honestly say that all Spiritualistic activities and all forms of Psychical Research are illegal, those interested in such subjects would at least know where they stand and engage in them at their own risk. But the Government does not do this. It publicly announces that Spiritualists need have no fear of any action being taken against them, unless they are found to be impostors, but at the same time as it says this, by a form of mental terrorism it prevents such activities from taking place.

It was mental terrorism which forced the president of the Redhill church to sign a document promising that no further demonstrations of mediumship would be held in the building. The same form of pressure was used to force the civic authorities at Altrincham to forbid the Spiritualist meeting being held in the Town Hall, and on the Railway Company to force it to withdraw the posters advertising that this meeting was to take place. In neither case did the question of imposture arise. Far from protecting the public from such methods, the Government deliberately leaves Spiritualists in the intolerable position of not knowing from one day to another what action the law may take against them, or who may be its next victim.

Ever since the day when the Emperor Theodosius promulgated his famous decree that all citizens of the Roman Empire who did not accept the Christian faith were to be put to death, mental terrorism has been the weapon which that Church has used to subdue Europe to its will. Fear of eternal punishment in the fires of hell not only impelled the common people to provide the money which built up its wealth, but the same fear made Kings grant it lands and privileges, and Governments pass laws which gave it power. The rack, the thumbscrew, the stake, and every other conceivable form of torture, was used on those who disputed its sovereignty or disbelieved its creed. When Catholics were in power they persecuted Protestants. When Protestants were in power they persecuted Catholics. For centuries they have both persecuted Mediums.

The fact that a law which was placed on the Statute Book two hundred years ago, during a period of inhuman religious persecution, is still employed against a religious community to-day, shows clearly that the superstitious fears which the Church instilled into people's minds have not yet been eradicated. Whitehall is still bound in the chains of a dead past, and threatens with punishment those who have cast off these superstitions and think with more enlightened minds.

The real objective behind these prosecutions is the elimination of mediumship, the closing down of Spiritualist churches and societies, and the cessation of all forms of psychical research. Spiritualists themselves are not only quite capable, they are both anxious and willing, to expose any suspicion of fraud on the part of any medium, without the assistance of police, magistrates or judges, very few of whom have the slightest knowledge of the complex subject of mediumship in any of its many aspects. The ignorance which some of these people have displayed at recent prosecutions is indeed pathetic. As the law stands to-day mediums are convicted before trial. Guilt is taken for granted. The evidence of those best able to judge, namely, Spiritualists themselves, who have had experience in such matters, is brushed aside as worthless, and every effort made to abolish this flagrant injustice and obtain religious freedom for thousands of law-abiding citizens ends in failure.

One cannot but ask the question, why is this the case?

CHAPTER XV.

THE HIDDEN HAND.

AFTER the Government had blocked the Bill which had been introduced into the House of Commons in 1931, Sir Arthur Conan Doyle called on one of His Majesty's Ministers and protested strongly at the methods which had been adopted to prevent Spiritualists from obtaining the religious freedom they had claimed.

He reminded this member of the Government that the Bill had been drawn up at the suggestion, and with the approval, of Mr. Clynes, the Home Secretary, and that Mr. Clynes had given an assurance to the deputation which he had received —of which Sir Arthur had been a member— that it would be given the sympathetic consideration of the Government, and that no difficulty would be placed in the way of having the subject discussed in Parliament. In spite of that assurance, however, the Government Whips had been instructed to take measures to prevent the Bill from passing its second reading. The Minister, who himself had promised to support the Bill, admitted frankly that Sir Arthur had good cause for complaint, but justified the action of the Government by saying " You know as well as I do, Doyle, that no political party in this country can afford to offend the Roman Catholic vote."

That illuminating reply goes a long way towards answering the question with which I closed the previous chapter—why is it that the efforts of Spiritualists to obtain justice and freedom of religion never meet with success?

There has always been a conflict between the prophet and the priest. The prophet speaks with the voice of the Spirit, the priest with the voice of the Church. The prophet is the channel through whom the human race holds contact with those who have passed into higher realms of existence and who are able, through the greater knowledge and wisdom they have acquired, to guide those who follow them in the paths of spiritual progression. The priest does not possess that knowledge or wisdom any more than do those whom he professes to teach. A man may be an eminent theologian, he may know the doctrines and creeds of his Church by heart, he may accept these doctrines and creeds in their entirety, but with it all he may be completely ignorant of the true spiritual nature of man, the reason for his existence here on earth, or the kind of life which awaits him beyond the grave. Without that knowledge he is unfitted to be the mentor of his fellows.

Moreover, the priest is not a free agent. He is the representative of an institution which, over a period of centuries, has accumulated vast wealth and power, and he knows that his livelihood depends on that wealth and power remaining unimpaired. It is therefore in his interests to teach not what may be for the good of the individual but for the good of his Church. If he is honest he dare not depart from the official doctrines which he has accepted and solemnly promised to teach at his ordination. Were he to do so, he would not only be admitting that his Church was teaching what he considered to be false doctrines but he would also be confessing that he was obtaining his employment in its service under false pretences.

The priest is thus tied to a system of theology which fet ers the free use of his reason, and the history of religion is a continuous record of the unending struggle which has always been waged between these two forms of teaching—the voice of the spirit or the voice of man.

The voice of the spirit was heard on the Day of Pentecost. On that occasion twelve men, followers of Jesus of Nazareth, while sitting together under conditions which all Spiritualists know to be favourable for such manifestations, were suddenly " filled with the spirit." In modern language, they went into a state of trance and were controlled by spirits from the Unseen World. The writer of the story gives details of that incident which any Spiritualist, who has experienced similar phenomena, can corroborate as happening to-day. The " rushing mighty wind " and the " tongues of fire " have their counterpart in the direct voice seance room of modern times. The words spoken through the lips of these simple uneducated men were in languages which they could not have understood and had probably never even heard of. Who spoke them ? They were spoken by the voice of the spirit, each spirit speaking in his own language, and through the mediumship of these twelve men spreading abroad " the wonderful works of God " to the multitude which had gathered round to listen. Some of the stupid elements of that crowd sarcastically exclaimed " these men are drunk," just as equally stupid people to-day say " mediums are all frauds." Intelligent people know better than to say silly things like that.

Other similar occurrences, though less spectacular, are recorded in the book of " The Acts of the Apostles," and until the third century the voice of the spirit prevailed throughout the early Christian church. As the teachings of Jesus were spread abroad people gathered themselves into communities, or churches, in which His followers accepted the principles He taught and carried out the ministrations of the spirit which had been the outstanding feature of His life and that of His disciples. The apostle Paul had placed on record the various gifts of the spirit with which the leaders of these churches should be endowed. Some, he said, possessed the gift of healing the sick, others possessed the gift of discerning spirits—that is to say, they were clairvoyant. Others were able to speak in divers kinds of tongues, as on the Day of Pentecost, obviously in a state of trance. These people were the " prophets " of the early Church, or, as they were sometimes called in those days, " the organs of the spirit "—a term which clearly indicates that the part they played in church services was that of being the instrument through whom spirit teaching was imparted to the people from the Unseen World.

That "signs and wonders" were performed not only by Jesus and His immediate disciples but by many of the early apostles is well known to any reader of the New Testament. But the Christian church has always taught that such incidents were "miracles," something beyond the bounds of natural law which could not be explained and must therefore have been performed by a special intervention of God. Why God should have chosen to intervene in this extraordinary manner in the affairs of the human race, in one particular locality and at that particular period of its history, but never before or since, is a question which the Church has never attempted to answer. It merely states dogmatically that such is the case, and even maintains that all similar incidents which took place at other periods of human history were, and still are, the work of the devil.

The absurdity of such an attitude towards what, in these modern days, is looked upon by all intelligent people as an every-day occurrence is demonstrated by the words of Jesus, that His followers would "do greater works than these" which He, Himself, had done. He did not restrict this power to any one period or place. Signs and wonders were a common feature in the lives of the early Christians ; they accepted them as such just as Spiritualists accept them to-day. If such things no longer form part of the teaching and practice of the Christian church the only explanation can be that the church has changed.

The priest has failed to carry on the work of the prophet.

The book of " The Acts of the Apostles " tells us, by its very name, that it was never completed. It is only the history of the very beginnings of the early Christian church. The term " apostle " cannot logically be applied only to the small group of men and women whose names we happen to read of in the New Testament. It applies to the leaders of the church prior to the Council of Nicea in the year 325. After that date sundry doctrines and beliefs, hitherto unknown among the early Christian communities, were introduced to satisfy the demands of other religions then existing throughout the Roman Empire. These religions were incorporated into Christianity on the orders of the Emperor Constantine, and the Church became a State Institution in which the ministry of the spirit was supplanted by the ministry of the priest. " The gifts of the spirit," says Principal Cairns in his book, " The Faith that Rebels," " gradually ceased because the Church got out of touch with the pure grace of God."

The priest took the place of the prophet.

But this sweeping revolution in the constitution of the Church did not take place without a bitter struggle on the part of those who desired the retention of the simple forms of earlier years. Much innocent blood was destined to flow before the priests eventually won the day. One of the outstanding names in the history of this struggle is that of Montanus, an early Christian who was strongly opposed to any form of Church government which eliminated the medium from his, or her, rightful place in the services of the Church. In his efforts to retain the original form of worship he was supported by a large following, including two women of high social position, Priscilla and Maximilla. These women, it would appear, were endowed with psychic gifts, as they both claimed to speak with the voice of the spirit, which gave the true message to the people, while the voice of the priest spoke only what he believed to be true. And, doubtless, human nature being what it is, he not infrequently spoke what suited his purpose, irrespective of whether it was true or not.

The Montanists, as they came to be called, believed in the constancy within the Church of supernormal phenomena. They maintained that prophetic—or mediumistic—utterances were an integral part of its teaching and that only those who were sufficiently gifted to be able to dispense this form of ministration should be looked upon as the genuine successors of the early apostles. This, in itself, aroused the anger of the priests, whose one object was to overthrow the original prophetic element in the Church and usurp the influence of the medium by taking all forms of church ministration into their own hands. A large number of the more prominent members of the early Church allied themselves to the Montanist movement, which spread widely throughout many parts of the Roman Empire both in Asia and Africa, where Tertullian joined its ranks. Even the Council of Nicea failed to put an end to its activities. It was not finally defeated by priestly power until the sixth century, although Montanus and his followers had been excommunicated by

Eleutherus, Bishop of Rome, and a number of Church Councils had issued threats of a similar penalty to those who still persisted in accepting the voice of the spirit instead of that of the priests.

Among the writings of the early Christian Fathers there are many references to the existence of true spiritual power within the churches. Mediumship formed as much a part of an early Christian church service as it does in a Spiritualist church to-day. Members of a present-day congregation in a Christian church have read to them the 14th chapter of 1st Corinthians, in which Paul gives some sound advice regarding the manner in which the churches should conduct their services " decently and in order." But how many of those listening to these words understand what they mean? " I would that ye all spake with tongues but rather that ye prophesied," reads the parson, but what do these words convey to the average church-goer? " Tongues are for a sign, not to them that believe but to them that believe not," and again, " If anything be revealed to another that sitteth by, let the first hold his peace." These exhortations, and others of a similar nature which this chapter contains, are understood by the Spiritualist, but in an orthodox church they might as well be read in the original Greek for all they convey to the uncomprehending listener in the pew.

That they were understood by the early Christians is certain. Irenaeus, writing at the beginning of the 3rd century, speaks of " many brethren in the church who possess prophetic gifts and speak through the spirit in all kinds of tongues."

Incidentally, the Church made Irenaeus a " saint."
If he and many of his contemporaries among the
Fathers of the Church lived to-day they would be
prosecuted under the Witchcraft Act. Tatian
relates how " our virgins utter divine oracles,
see visions and sing holy words that are given to
them." Tertullian, to whom I have already
referred, writes in " De Anima "—" To-day there
is among us a sister who has received gifts in the
nature of revelations, which she experiences in the
church amid the rites of the Lord's Day, falling
into ecstasy. She converses with angels, sees and
hears mysteries, reads the hearts of certain people
and brings healing to those who ask." Tertullian
further records how this medium (as she would be
called to-day) had said " A soul was shown to me
in bodily form, it seemed as if it might be touched,
of human form in every detail."

I need only give one further example. Augustine,
another of the Church's " saints," tells us that
" the spirits of the dead can be sent to the living
and can unveil to them the future." And again,
" I call them prophets who, being out of themselves
and their own thoughts, did utter forth whatsoever
the impelling power of the spirit wrought in them,
while the Divine Operator served Himself of them
and their organs, even as men do of a trumpet."

The men who wrote these words, and many
others who wrote in a similar strain regarding the
existence and activities of mediums in the early
Christian church, were among the leaders of that
Church, which has honoured them for centuries as
the witnesses through whom the truths of

Christianity were preserved and handed down to their successors. But if these writings contain the truths of Christianity, why have they always been suppressed in the Church's teaching? Would any clergyman at the present day dare to include one of these quotations in his sermon? If he had the courage to do so, and followed it up by a demonstration of clairvoyance, or " discerning of spirits," as he would probably prefer to call it, his church would soon be filled to overflowing. He, himself, however, would soon find himself dismissed from his charge.

And so these truths, which every scholar of Church history must know, are carefully hidden away and kept from the ears and eyes of a generation which has discarded its belief in out-worn theologies, and is desperately longing to find some solid facts on which to base its spiritual life. But, no! the priest has supplanted the prophet. For sixteen hundred years he has held the whip-hand and kept the prophet in subjection. He has tortured him, deported him, burned him, and has harried him from one end of Christendom to the other. It is not likely that he will now vacate the position of ease and security he has won without fighting to the last ditch to preserve it. If only it were a clean fight Spiritualists would welcome it. But our opponents dare not come out into the open. Their attacks never come from the front, only from behind.

Many of the so-called " saints " of the Christian church were mediums. St. Joan, St. Catherine of Bologna, St. Catherine of Siena, St. Theresa, to name only a few, were both clairvoyant and clairaudient. Others possessed the gift of healing. Oliver Leroy, in his treatise on Levitation, states that over 200 " saints " were known to have experienced this particular form of phenomena. A peasant girl named Bernadette Soubirous, in 1858, clairvoyantly saw a spirit form which she believed to be the Virgin Mary, who told her of the healing powers of the celebrated spring at Lourdes. Fortunately for her she was a Roman Catholic, and she told a priest what she had seen. If she had been a Spiritualist medium she would probably have been told that she had seen the devil ! In " The History of Spiritualism," Sir Arthur Conan Doyle writes—" The Roman Catholic church has most illogically stigmatised as diabolism in others that which it has claimed as a special mark of sanctity in itself. The *Acta Sanctorum* are one long chronicle of psychic phenomena with levitations, apports, prophecy, and all the other signs of mediumistic power. This Church, however, has always persecuted Spiritualism."

In my earlier book, " The Unbroken Melody of Life," I record a conversation I once had with a Roman Catholic priest, in which he condemned Spiritualism in the strongest terms. But when I asked him to explain certain experiences which had convinced me of the truth of spirit communication, he replied " We in the Church know perfectly well that such things happen, but it would never do to let the people know that ! "

There spoke the voice of the priest. And millions of devout Catholics consider the voice of the priest to be the voice of God. In fact, if the words of Pope Innocent III. mean anything at all, they mean that, in the eyes of the Church, the priest is superior to God. According to this pope, " Christ died to institute the priesthood. . . . In obedience to the words of the priest, ' *Hoc est corpus meum*,' God Himself comes whenever called and places Himself in the priests' hands. And having come He remains entirely at their disposal. They can move Him as they please ; they can shut Him up in the tabernacle ; they can carry Him outside the church. God Himself is obliged to abide by the judgment of His priests, and either pardon or not, according as they give absolution or refuse it." This quotation is taken from " The Papal Conquest " by Dr. Alexander Robertson of Venice, who adds this comment, " Anyone who believes this monstrous thing is henceforth entirely at the mercy of the priest. His eternal destiny is in his hands."

But the voice of one priest is not always the voice of another. The Church of Rome is an expert in the art of subtlety and craftiness. What it says for the ears of the Protestant is vastly different to what it says for the edification of the faithful. In this way it has managed to disarm suspicion and burrow its way into almost every corner of public life, where it carries on its deceptions and intrigues, always directed to one end—the overthrow of every obstacle which stands in the way of it regaining full liberty and power over the souls and bodies of the people. Listen, for example, to Cardinal Wiseman, as he addresses

Queen Victoria in the name of the Catholics of
England :—

> " In whatever our Church has at any time
> done for establishing its system of government
> among its members in this island, we beg most
> fervently and most sincerely to assure your
> Majesty that the organisation granted to us is
> entirely ecclesiastical and its authority purely
> spiritual. It leaves untouched every tittle of
> your Majesty's rights, authority, power,
> jurisdiction, and prerogative as our sovereign
> and as sovereign over these realms."

Could anything sound more loyal or more
reasonable ? Doubtless the tones of his voice as he
uttered these words were sweet as honey. And no
doubt his listeners, or some of them, believed that
he was speaking the truth. But listen now to his
brother-priest, Cardinal Manning, who a few years
later is instructing his flock in the mighty powers
which are invested in his Church, and in himself
as its administrator in England :—

> " If an heretical prince is elected, or succeeds
> to the throne, the Church has a right to say
> ' I annul the election, or I forbid the succession.'
> Again, if a king of a Christian nation falls into
> heresy he commits an offence against God. . . .
> Therefore it is in the power of the Church, in
> virtue of the supreme authority with which she
> is vested by Christ over all Christian men, to
> depose such a prince in punishment of his
> spiritual crime. . . . Moreover, the right

of deposing kings is inherent in the supreme sovereignty which the Pope, as viceregent of Christ, exercises over all Christian nations. . . . When, therefore, the Head of the Church exercises his supreme authority either by excommunicating individuals, by laying nations under an interdict, or by deposing kings, all Christian people are bound to obey his decree."

Now, these two statements are obviously contradictory. One of them is untrue. Knowing the Roman church as we do, with its claims and ambitions, Cardinal Wiseman was clearly, in the words of the Vagrancy Act, " using subtle craft " in order to " deceive and impose on Her Majesty's subjects." If the law were impartial he would have been declared " a rogue and a vagabond " and been either fined or sent to prison. But he was a priest of the Roman Catholic church, not a Spiritualist medium. That makes all the difference !

The Church of Rome hates Spiritualism. It is its deadliest enemy. It hates it because it fears it. If Spiritualists were merely frauds or fools, as some of their opponents declare them to be, Rome could afford to ignore them. Rome knows better than anybody else that Spiritualism is not fraud. It knows it is the Truth. And because it is the Truth, Rome is prepared to go to any lengths, by fair means or foul, to discredit it in the eyes of the public, in the hope that by so doing it will force it out of existence.

The Protestant churches are living in a fool's paradise. They little realise the extent to which Roman Catholicism is steadily eating its way into the heart of the nation. The Church of England is honeycombed with Roman Catholic priests, treacherously and insidiously instilling into the minds of the people the doctrines and dogmas of their creed. Ritual and ceremonial play a definite part in the Anglican form of worship. This provides a suitable breeding ground in which the seeds of Romanism can successfully be sown. In many different ways the Protestant churches are playing into the hands of Rome, and not least is this the case in their attitude towards Spiritualism. Like the Church of Rome they know that Spiritualism is true. They know that communication with the departed is an established fact. They know that its claims and teaching are founded upon fact. But they refuse to admit this knowledge. Instead, they stand by, silent and aloof, and by doing so they are not only emptying their own churches but they are encouraging the subversive activities of the " hidden hand," embodied in the Church to which Mr. Gladstone referred in his famous pamphlet, " Vaticanism," when he wrote " My object has been to produce a temper of greater watchfulness . . . to warn my countrymen against the velvet paw, the smooth and soft exterior of a system which is dangerous to the foundations of civil order."

To such an extent has Spiritualism spread during recent years, and so widely is it being discussed by both clergy and laity, that in 1937 a committee was appointed by Dr. Cosmo Lang, then

Archbishop of Canterbury, to inquire into the subject.
The object of the committee, it was officially stated,
was "to investigate the subject of communications
with discarnate spirits and the claims of Spiritualism
in relation to the Christian faith," and its chairman,
Dr. Underhill, Bishop of Bath and Wells, affirmed
that "its sole aim is to arrive at the truth." That
may have been, and doubtless was, Dr. Underhill's
personal desire and intention, as he himself was
not only convinced of the truth of Spiritualism,
but it was through him and the Rev. G. Maurice
Elliott that the request for the appointment of the
committee was made. But subsequent events
suggest very clearly that "truth" would only be
considered as "truth" if the findings of the
committee suited the convenience of Dr. Lang and
the bishops of the Church. Should they be otherwise,
that is, favourable to Spiritualism, the activities of
the committee were to be brought to an end and
no explanations given. That is what actually
took place.

The committee investigated its subject thoroughly
and impartially for over two years. Its members
attended seances, sat with well-known mediums,
interviewed prominent Spiritualists, and after
reaching its conclusion it presented its report to
the Primate. Seven members signed a majority
report stating that, in their opinion, the claims
of Spiritualism are true. It is only right that their
names should be known. They were :—

    Dr. Francis Underhill. Bishop of Bath and
    Wells.

Canon Anson, Master of the Temple.

Dr. W. R. Matthews, Dean of St. Paul's.

Canon L. W. Grensted, Examining Chaplain to the Archbishop of York.

Dr. William Brown, the eminent Psychologist.

Mr. P. E. Sandlands, K.C.

Lady (Gwendolen) Stephenson.

The three members who signed a minority report included Dr. Underhill's secretary and the wife of the Bishop of Derby. They did not condemn the findings of their colleagues or express any antagonistic views on the subject. They merely "reserved their opinion," as they did not feel justified in publicly declaring that they had been fully convinced.

It had naturally been expected that the report of this committee would be published after it had been perused by the Archbishop of Canterbury. Its work had not been kept secret. Thousands of clergymen and members of the general public throughout the country were awaiting its decisions with eagerness. But to everybody's intense astonishment the report was suppressed. When appealed to, Dr. Lang instructed his chaplain to reply, "It is not proposed at present to publish the report. When it came up for review it was felt that further investigation was required, and that premature publication would be liable to give rise to misunderstanding."

Now, that reply raises one or two interesting points. In the first place it says that it is not proposed to publish the report " at present." That was over six years ago and nothing more has been heard of it since. It then goes on to say that "further investigation was required." This further investigation has never taken place. The committee's chairman, Dr. Underhill, had stated that the sole aim of the committee was "to arrive at the truth." Presumably, therefore, he and his colleagues who signed the majority report in favour of Spiritualism were satisfied that they *had* arrived at the truth. If they were not satisfied on this vital point why did they sign the report? Why was a report sent in at all, if it did not contain what the signatories considered to be "the truth?" Again, why should its publication "give rise to misunderstanding?" If any statements in the report were obscure or not readily understood, it would have been a simple matter to have had these statements re-written in such a way as to make them clear. Any lawyer will agree that many Acts of Parliament "give rise to misunderstanding." They can be read in more ways than one. But that does not prevent them from being placed on the Statute Book and becoming the law of the land.

Obviously, this reply was merely an excuse. The report was favourable to Spiritualism, so Dr. Lang and the Bishops decided that it should be withheld from publication. This decision aroused a storm of protest. Many prominent people, including members of the committee itself, openly expressed their disapproval in the strongest terms, but in spite of that the report remains, and is likely to remain indefinitely, in some dusty pigeon-hole in Lambeth Palace, safely hidden from the public gaze. On the other hand, had the report condemned Spiritualism and upheld orthodox teaching concerning the after-life, one cannot help wondering if the same secrecy would have been maintained.

If any doubt exists as to the determination of the orthodox churches to do everything in their power to prevent freedom in the public expression of any religious beliefs, except their own, this is dispelled by their attitude towards the broadcasting of religious services by the B.B.C. In earlier days, if anyone were interested in some particular subject, he could only study it by means of books or, if he were fortunate enough to live in a city, by attending lectures or discussions among those whose interests were similar to his own. If he lived in the country this latter opportunity was denied him. The coming of wireless has altered this state of affairs. Anyone living in the remotest hamlet can now switch on his wireless set and listen to whatever he wishes to hear.

But in saying this I must emphasise one very important exception, namely, Religion. In this country religion is the one subject on which free expression of opinion is not allowed in our wireless programmes. That is a monopoly held by the Christian churches.

It has been calculated that only between five and ten per cent. of the members of orthodox churches ever attend any form of church service. Even on Easter Sunday, when all members of the Church of England are supposed to partake of the sacrament of Holy Communion, only about ten per cent. of the total

17

membership of that denomination attend church. On other Sundays it is considerably less. But outside the ranks of orthodoxy there are millions of people who belong to other religions or accept other forms of religious belief. For these the B.B.C. does not allow any religious instruction to be provided. They must either listen to the teachings of orthodoxy or not listen at all.

The responsibility for this dogmatic attitude rests on a committee known as the Religious Advisory Committee of the B.B.C. This committee consists of a number of clergymen representing a few of the larger denominations of the orthodox churches. It is their duty to arrange that part of the weekly wireless programme devoted to subjects of a religious nature. They decide among themselves who, and what denomination, will be allowed the use of the microphone and the length of time to be allotted to each. The B.B.C. itself is supposed to be undenominational in religion as it is non-party in politics. Officially, it is a neutral organisation and, like any other National institution, it should be run for the benefit of the general public, irrespective of creed, religious or otherwise.

Apparently the members of the Religious Advisory Committee are under the impression that the only people who take out wireless licences and pay their annual subscription for the privilege of using a wireless set are members of the orthodox churches. Their decision is that, as this is (nominally) a Christian country, only those who accept this particular form of religious creed need to be catered for, despite the fact that Dr. Chavasse,

Bishop of Rochester, has sorrowfully admitted that " it is impossible to exaggerate the gulf which exists between the Church and the life and thinking of English people." This decision is a deliberate stifling of the freedom to give public expression to religious opinion. The attitude of the Religious Advisory Committee is in direct opposition to the much vaunted " Freedom of Religion " expressed in the Atlantic Charter, for which, among other things, we have been fighting this war.

Spiritualists are not the only people affected by the banning of free religious speech on the wireless. Vast numbers of people throughout the country, who profess religions other than Christian, are equally debarred from hearing their own form of church service, simply because the members of the Religious Advisory Committee of the B.B.C. disapprove of it. The beliefs of other people differ from their's, therefore other people must suffer.

Judging by the size of the congregations in Spiritualist churches and the crowds which attend a Spiritualist service held in any of the largest halls of our great cities (including those who are frequently turned away for lack of accommodation) it is a conservative estimate to say that at least a million people in this country are either Spiritualists by religious profession or are interested in the subject. A few years ago one of our leading daily newspapers estimated the number at three millions, but I am content to uphold the justice of our case on one-third of that number. Then there are several hundred thousand Unitarians, Jews, Christian Scientists,

to name only a few, while, under the heading of
" Other Religions " a recent edition of *Whitaker's
Almanack* gives a total of 3,800,000 persons in
England, Scotland and Wales.

Now, Christians are not the only people who
pay for a wireless licence each year. The B.B.C.
is supported and financed by people of all shades
of religious opinion who are entitled to the same
treatment as are members of the various sects of
orthodoxy. They do not ask for an equal share
with the Christian community in the matter of
Sunday evening services, but they do maintain
that they are entitled to hear one of their own
services broadcast occasionally. Those who do not
wish to listen need not do so. There is always an
alternative programme at their disposal on which,
if demand justified it, an orthodox service could be
relayed either at the same time or at a different
hour on the same evening. To say, as the Religious
Advisory Committee does, that *only* orthodox
services should be broadcast because the *majority*
of people in this country profess Christianity
would mean, if carried to its logical conclusion,
that only Church of England services should be
broadcast because the majority of Christians in
this country belong to that particular sect. Would
the non-Anglican members of the Religious Advisory
Committee agree to that ? If not, they have no
right to penalise others in a way they would not be
prepared to be penalised themselves.

The policy of the committee is clearly, if
unconsciously, exposed in the words of the present
Dean of St. Paul's, who recently said " Institutional

religion does not represent the gospel of Christ but the opinions of a mass of nominal Christians. It cannot be expected to do more than look after its own interests and reflect the ideas of its supporters." Very true. Its monopoly over all religious broadcasting in this country certainly enables it to " look after its own interests," but what of the millions of listeners who are not interested in " Institutional religion " or in " the ideas of its supporters," and who strongly object to being deprived of their own forms of religious teaching on the wireless, and having " the opinions of a mass of nominal Christians " incessantly dinned into their ears instead ?

An earnest and conscientious Unitarian, for example, is as worthy of consideration by the B.B.C. as a " nominal " Christian, but he receives none. Florence Nightingale was a Unitarian. The members of the Religious Advisory Committee would, no doubt, be among the first to pay tribute to her self-sacrificing life and example, but if the B.B.C. had existed in those days and Florence Nightingale had wanted to express her firm conviction that true religion consisted in forgetting self and ministering to the needs of others, that would have been forbidden because her religious beliefs did not conform to the Christian creed !

A few years ago the National Council of the Spiritualists' National Union endeavoured to arrange for a Spiritualist church service being broadcast on a Sunday evening. I was a member of the National Council at the time, and as I write I have before me a copy of the correspondence which passed

between us and the Rev. F. A. Iremonger, who
then held the post of Director of Religion in the
B.B.C. The correspondence is too long to quote
in full, but the request by the Spiritualists' National
Union was supported by detailed facts and figures
showing that Spiritualists were a body as large as,
if not larger than, many other non-conformist
denominations. After pointing out that the National
Council spoke for " a large and ever-growing body of
sincere people who accept Spiritualism as their
religion," the letter ended with the following
paragraph :—

> " As citizens of a country in which religious
> equality is rightly regarded as the birthright of
> every citizen, we ask that you acknowledge and
> give effect to this position. May we draw your
> attention to the remarks of Lord Hewart, the
> Lord Chief Justice, in his summing-up of a case
> in July, 1935, in which this Union was awarded
> £1,500 damages for libel :—' How far
> Spiritualism should, or should not, adopt the
> tenets of the Christian religion and those
> topics, whatever they are, are better discussed
> in the bracing air at a conference in Blackpool.
> You and I are not concerned with them ;
> nor is it right to look with scorn upon the whole
> theory and practice of Spiritualism. We are
> told that it is a religion. There is no credit
> in being tolerant about one's own religion.
> They are entitled, are they not, to fair play ?
> They ask for no more, they ought to have
> no less."

The B.B.C. does not admit that Spiritualism is entitled to fair play, so the Religious Advisory Committee replied regretting that it was unable to agree to a Spiritualist service being broadcast. Dr. Iremonger wrote :—

"You will, we are sure, understand that the number of requests to broadcast services which we receive is very large, and that the committee has had to lay down certain principles by which it is guided in granting or refusing these requests. The most important of these principles is that, before a request for an evening service is granted, the committee shall have satisfied itself that the teaching of the applying body is such as can be said to be in the main stream of Christian tradition."

On hearing this letter read the members of the National Council were puzzled as to the exact meaning of the phrase "in the main stream of Christian tradition," and our secretary was instructed to write and ask for these words to be more precisely defined.

Now, surely that was a reasonable request and one which any reasonable body of men would readily grant. Moreover, could any better opportunity have been given for making a brief and concise statement of the main tenets of the Christian faith? Obviously, the doctrines considered as essential and held in common by the Church of England, the Church of Scotland, the Free Churches and the Church of Rome comprise "the main stream of Christian tradition," as all of these denominations are permitted regularly to broadcast religious teaching. What a chance this was for Roman Catholics and Protestants, members of one committee and met together as a band of Christian brothers, to have spoken with one united voice and given to the world their common creed! It would have been an epoch-making Confession of a Common Faith by the representatives of the largest sects of the Christian church.

But the Religious Advisory Committee was unequal to the task. A golden opportunity was lost, and instead of complying with our request they merely replied with the usual stereotyped formula that they had nothing further to add to their previous letter.

The Christian churches have always maintained that their religion was founded by Jesus Christ and was a direct revelation from God. Now we know on the authority of the religious experts of the B.B.C. that this is not the case. It is merely a "tradition." What lies within the "main stream" of that tradition and what lies outside it nobody knows, and unfortunately our advisers on religious matters are either unable or unwilling to enlighten us on the subject. According to the dictionary the word "tradition" means the "handing down of opinions from ancestors to posterity." Spiritualism is not interested in tradition where religious teaching is concerned. True religion does not depend on tradition any more than human life depends on the history of the past. History does not constitute human life. Tradition does not constitute true religion.

This episode, like that of the suppression of the report of Dr. Lang's committee, still further emphasises the fact that there is a " hidden hand " at work, prepared to use every means at its disposal to prevent the teachings of Spiritualism being given to the people, while the banning of Spiritualist services by the police and the systematic prosecution of mediums under two antiquated Acts of Parliament leave no doubt that its ultimate object is to drive Spiritualism out of existence. Those responsible for these reactionary methods should remember the legendary story of King Canute, who foolishly tried to stop the inflow of the waves of the sea. History will record that their efforts were no more successful than his were. Truth can be retarded but not destroyed.

" If this work be of men it will come to nought, but if it be of God ye cannot overthrow it." With these words in their minds, and with the knowledge that behind them are unseen hosts of spirit helpers, Spiritualists carry on.

CHAPTER XVI.

FACE THE FACTS.

IN the foregoing pages I have endeavoured to give a brief outline of Spiritualism—its claims, its beliefs and the forces that are arrayed against it. I must now leave the reader to judge whether the subject is worthy of further study, or not.

No one can make a person become a Spiritualist simply by writing books about it. Books, lectures and discussions may all play their part in arousing interest in the subject. They may bring to people something of the experiences of others and perhaps awaken in them a desire to investigate the matter for themselves. But it is only by personal investigation, carried on, it may be, over a lengthy period of time, that conviction can be achieved. We do not ask people merely to *believe*, we ask them to find out for themselves, so that they can say beyond all shadow of doubt that they *know* the claims of Spiritualism are true.

It is a vast subject. It may be considered in either its scientific or its religious aspect. In either case it offers a wide field for interesting and profitable study. Even now the most experienced Spiritualist will admit that only the fringe of the subject has been touched, only the surface scratched.

Columbus discovered America, but many generations, even centuries, had to come and go before that great continent became what it is to-day. And even now parts of it still remain unexplored.

When some primitive man, in the early days of the world's history, conceived the idea of hollowing out the trunk of a tree and thus making for himself a rude boat in which he might venture on the sea, he little thought that he was the fore-runner of the builders of a " Queen Mary " or " Queen Elizabeth." The first crude craft from which men shot their arrows was the progenitor of the modern battleship, capable of travelling at a speed of over thirty knots and flinging destruction to a distance of over twenty miles from its 16-inch guns.

Modern Spiritualism, as it is called, was born in a humble cottage. Its first mediums were two young girls who unconsciously acted as the trans-mitter between the Spirit World and ours. A very insignificant beginning. To all appearances a trifling incident not worthy of more than passing notice. But from that small seed there has grown a mighty tree of knowledge which is destined to grow until all peoples of the world find security and comfort under its branches.

Spiritualism must continue to grow. It is rooted in soil which is neither creed nor tradition, but definitely proved facts. People in their ignorance may jeer at these facts, they may persuade themselves and try to persuade others that such things do not happen, they may know they happen and do their utmost to hide them from their fellow men and women. But, sooner or later, the truths of Spiritualism will be looked upon as part of general every-day knowledge and will be accepted as readily as any other common fact of nature is accepted to-day.

How often, when a Spiritualist relates some experience he has had, which confirms the truth that communication between the two worlds is possible, does he receive the reply "how amazing!" or "it sounds incredible!" There is nothing either amazing or incredible about it. Death is as much an ordinary process of nature as birth; in fact, death *is* birth—the birth of the spirit body into another realm of existence. Only the physical body is left behind. The real "ego" still lives, not in some far off distant heaven among "redeemed" souls who float about as vapoury wraiths, and whose interest in this world has ceased to exist, but as a real and tangible individual with memory, love and all mental qualities unimpaired. All the more vibrant with life because the limitations of the physical body have been laid aside.

Why should these living, loving and thinking beings beyond the veil be separated from our ken? Only ignorance makes people believe this must be the case. The normal physical eye is unable to see them, and the ear to hear their voice, but in ordinary daily life these limitations do not prevent communication between us and our friends. Nobody expresses astonishment when some one living in, say, Edinburgh says to another "I was speaking to so-and-so in London last night." But the person who had made that remark a hundred years ago would have been considered mad. To-day the telephone is an instrument which is in daily and hourly use. It has long ago ceased to be either amazing or incredible.

Some years ago, when crossing the Atlantic from New York, I spoke to my mother by telephone from about 500 miles off the Irish coast. I told her the hour at which we expected to dock in Glasgow and asked her to arrange for my car being at the quay-side to meet me. After I had laid down the receiver in the wireless room of the " Transylvania " I thought no more about it. On our arrival I found the car waiting for me and was home, twenty miles from Glasgow, within an hour of setting foot ashore. Wasn't it amazing ? Incredible ? Yes, fifty years ago it would have been impossible, but thanks to radio-telephony and the motor car such an incident is now an every-day occurrence. My mother was far beyond the range of my sight and hearing, but I spoke to her over 500 miles of watery space by means of an instrument —the telephone. We speak to those who have passed on to the other side of life also by means of an instrument—the medium. The only difference is that they are not 500 miles away from us but actually with us, although unless we possess the psychic faculty ourselves we do not realise their presence.

It is all a question of getting accustomed to something new.

Centuries of wrong teaching has impressed upon our minds the conviction that the so-called dead are beyond our reach ; it has even taught us that to attempt to reach them is sin. Put aside prejudice and consider the matter dispassionately. What authority has any person for saying that it is either impossible or wrong to make contact with those who have passed on? Do such people know any more about the subject than those whom they censure so strongly? Invariably they know a great deal less!

I have heard the voice of Mr. Gladstone twice since he left this world. Earlier in this book I have recorded how he spoke at a direct-voice seance and gave certain evidence of his continued existence which was acknowledged as correct. The other occasion was when, as a boy, I put a penny in the slot of a new-fangled instrument called a phonograph and heard his voice recorded on a wax cylinder. At least, a notice above the phonograph stated " Put a penny in the slot and hear the voice of Mr. Gladstone." Doubtless many people did so and accepted the voice as genuine. Perhaps it was, perhaps it wasn't, but there was not the slightest vestige of evidence to support the statement. Yet people did not wreck the phonograph for being a " fraud " or think it wicked to indulge in this innocent form of entertainment. But I wonder how many of these same people would believe me if I told them that Mr. Gladstone had spoken, not through a wax cylinder, but with his own voice at a seance and had given convincing evidence that it really was he who was speaking.

As a matter of common sense and critical judgment the occasion on which he did give evidence that the voice was his is of infinitely greater value than the occasion on which he did not give this evidence. I can say I *know* I have heard the voice of Mr. Gladstone. The others who heard the phonograph record can only say " I believe."

I do not claim that the incidents I have narrated in this book, which first convinced me and then confirmed my conviction that the claims of Spiritualism are true, are in any way unique. I do not even claim that the evidence adduced in every case is absolutely water-tight. The critic will doubtless find in some of them flaws and loopholes which enable him to explain them away to his own satisfaction. But, taking them as a whole, they contain as much, and as good, evidence in favour of the case in point as that produced in any court of law. Many a person has been convicted on much less. How, for example, does the critic explain the incident described in Chapter X. dealing with the flower placed in my mother's hand after her death? Only one person in the world knew that had been done, and she was twenty miles away from the place where my brother and I were sitting with Mrs. Harris. To suggest that it was due to telepathy is surely a grotesque assertion. And even telepathy—that last ditch of the unbelieving die-hard—cannot explain how Mrs. Harris was able to assure us that in a certain article of furniture, containing " one small drawer," there were papers and letters which had been put there by my mother without anybody's knowledge. I am convinced, as the result of the inquiries my brother and I subsequently made, that no person living on earth knew that drawer existed, still less what it contained.

If it was not my wife who told Mr. Shields that I was ill, who was it ? It was an utter impossibility that this news could have reached Glasgow before the seance commenced. My wife spoke in her own voice which was heard by all present, not through the lips of any medium. How could Mrs. Larder describe accurately my friend, " Wyck " McCready, as standing beside me dressed in yachting garb, when I did not even know he had died ? Who told Mrs. Dowds on 25th February, 1942, that my son had escaped from Burma only forty-eight hours before and that he was " on the sea," the last place anybody would have expected him to be? Questions such as these have to be faced and answered. Before the claims of Spiritualism are rejected they must be answered in a reasonable and convincing manner. Vague theories and speculations are not enough. The opposition must prove its case.

In relating these incidents there is one form of psychic phenomena which I have not so far mentioned. That is Materialisation. I have attended a number of such seances and have seen many spirit forms fully materialised and recognised by those present. On one occasion, when visiting Aberdeen, my friend, Mr. Herbert Hill, president of the Spiritualist Church there, took me to a materialisation seance which was held in the house of one of the members of his church. I had never been in Aberdeen before, and, beyond the fact that I had spoken in the church the previous day, I was quite unknown to my host and hostess and

to the other people present.   At that seance
fourteen discarnate individuals living in the Spirit
World materialised so that they could be seen by
their relatives and friends living on earth.   Their
bodies were solid, their features exact in every
detail.   One man gazed into the eyes of his
" dead " brother and then said " There is no doubt
about it.   Nobody else ever had eyelashes like that."
A woman who materialised spoke to her daughter,
then, after looking round the room, she inquired why
her other daughter was not there.   She was told
that she had been prevented from coming at the
last moment and was asked if she would care to
write her a note.   On a small table lay a writing-
pad and a pencil.   The woman picked these up and
wrote.   After the seance was over her daughter let
me see what was written—a few words of greeting—
and assured me that it was in her mother's hand-
writing.

It was at that seance that my wife materialised
for the first time since she had passed on.   I
recognised her instantly.   After a few words had
passed between us she said " I want to come right
under the light so that you can be sure it really is
myself."   There was a red light suspended from the
ceiling in the centre of the room.   The sitters moved
their chairs aside and my wife walked under the
light and held up her face so that I could see it
distinctly.   Then she did what, to other people,
must have seemed a strange thing.   She drew back
her lips and pointed with her finger to her teeth.

Now, my wife's teeth were one of her outstanding
features.   I have heard her dentist say he had

18

never seen a more perfect set of natural teeth. She deliberately drew my attention to this feature as an item of evidential value. After the seance I took the earliest opportunity of looking carefully at the teeth of the medium. The less said about them the better ! Perhaps I should add that the medium had been stripped and every article of her clothing carefully searched by two ladies before she entered the seance room.

A few days later I had a sitting with a medium in London. The first words my wife said were " Tell me, did you see me quite plainly ? I was rather nervous, as it was the first time I had shown myself that way. It was a good idea my letting you see my teeth."

On a subsequent occasion, when she had become more accustomed to materialising her spirit body, she took an electric torch from one of the sitters and for a few moments played the light over her face. Well, either it was my wife or it wasn't. It certainly was not the medium, who bore not the slightest resemblance to her either in size or features. My mother has also materialised in a similar way, and has been recognised not only by myself but by two other sitters who had known her when she was on earth.

Again I say that such experiences are in no way unique. Comparatively few people may have had the opportunity of witnessing materialisations, especially under the exceptionally good conditions which I was privileged to enjoy, but tens of thousands of people in this country alone, and millions throughout the world, could relate at least one convincing experience in support of the truth that life persists after so-called death. Many could relate far more than I can. A few years ago Mr. Ernest Oaten, the editor of " The Two Worlds " and a past-president of the Spiritualists' National Union, published a book entitled " That Reminds Me." Its sub-title, " A Medlay of Personal Psychic Experiences," aptly describes its contents. Mr. Oaten could write another volume on the same subject any time he chose to do so and another one after that ! Half a century spent in the critical investigation of psychic phenomena yields a rich harvest, and few have garnered a richer harvest in that respect than Mr. Oaten. Yet there are ignorant and self-complacent people in the world, who would be scared stiff if they heard a spirit voice and die of fright if they saw a spirit form, who have never given the subject a moment's study, but who nevertheless reject all such accumulations of evidence as worthless and cast them aside as rubbish only fit to be thrown on the fire.

The value of such evidence is inestimable. It proves that death is not the end. It assures us beyond all doubt that life persists beyond the grave and that those whom we have loved and think we have lost are still our close companions. Ignorance begets fear. The mystery and fear of death have been like an unseen hand clutching the throat of humanity in the dark. Now that mystery exists no longer. Fear has turned to joy, because we know what lies before us and that death does not separate us from those we love.

To condemn Spiritualism on the ground that it is dangerous, as some people do, is sheer nonsense. Many things are dangerous if they are handled recklessly. Every month the B.B.C. and the newspapers tell us of the appalling loss of life on the roads. Does that mean that motor cars should be abolished? People meet with accidents on the railways. Should travel by train be prohibited? Electricity can kill you and gas can poison you, but that does not mean that we should live in a perpetual black-out or go back to the days when streets and houses were lit by tallow flares. Religious mania is one of the commonest forms of insanity. Would orthodox church-goers agree that churches should be done away with and parsons prohibited from preaching? The allegation that Spiritualism causes lunacy was completely refuted when, after a certain Dr. Forbes Winslow had made this statement in public, he was challenged by the Spiritualists' National Union to substantiate the charge. After making full and exhaustive inquiries in every conceivable quarter, Dr. Winslow acted as an honourable man and withdrew his remark, admitting it to be totally unfounded. His letter to that effect is still in the hands of the Union's officials.

In these days of bereavement and sorrow Spiritualism has been a consolation to thousands who otherwise would have been in despair. The orthodox churches have no message of comfort to give to the bereaved, only a vague hope of reunion at some unspecified future date. Spiritualism gives knowledge and brings the mourner into contact with the one whose physical body has been laid aside. Only a few days ago a medium whom I have known for many years, Miss Mary Buchanan, told me the following story.

She was conducting a service one week-day afternoon recently in one of the Glasgow Spiritualist churches. During her demonstration of clairvoyance she saw, standing beside a woman in the audience, the spirit of a young man in uniform. She described the spirit to the woman, gave the name which she received from him clairaudiently and told her that he was her son. The woman accepted these facts as correct and, after the service was over, expressed her deep gratitude to the medium for having given her this message. She told her that, only an hour or two before, she had been preparing to go out and do some household shopping when she had received the news that her son had been killed. As the shopping had to be done she had set out from her home, but going from shop to shop she hardly knew what she was doing or what she was buying. She was completely crushed by the blow that had fallen on her so suddenly. She knew nothing about Spiritualism, and the beliefs which she had been taught regarding death and the after-life failed to comfort her.

At last, while waiting to be served in a shop she had sat down, utterly exhausted, and burst into tears. One or two strangers gathered round, and when they heard her story tried to console her and sympathised with her as best they could. One of these strangers was a Spiritualist. Her sympathy took practical form. Tearing a leaf out of her note-book she wrote the address of the church at which she knew this afternoon service was being held. Giving it to the woman she said "Go to that address and ask for Miss Buchanan. I am sure she will be able to help you." Not knowing that she was going to a Spiritualist church the broken-hearted woman took the paper and hurried off, arriving just as the service was about to commence. When Miss Buchanan addressed her, describing her son and giving his name, she seemed dazed and unable to understand what was taking place. It was only afterwards, when it was explained to her that she had been at a Spiritualist service, and that her son was not "lost" to her but still with her and still able to speak to her, that her gratitude overflowed. "It is wonderful," she exclaimed to Miss Buchanan. "Why isn't everybody told about this?"

Miss Buchanan added that since that day she has frequently had the privilege of bringing that mother and son together. For that woman, as for thousands of others, Spiritualism has been the means whereby death has lost its sting and the grave its victory. That is the work of the devil, some say. Let them say it! It is the work of the angels.

I began this book by recounting how the "Daily Mail," some years ago, had instituted an inquiry into Spiritualism. Asked to express his opinion on the subject, Dr. Pollock, Bishop of Norwich, said "The Church has something better to offer." Dr. Scott Lidgett, the well-known non-conformist minister, said "It is not God's will that the veil hiding the life beyond should be drawn aside." I wonder if he had ever heard of what happened on the Mount of Transfiguration or of the resurrection of Jesus!

But if the Church really has "something better to offer," it is legitimate to ask why it does not do so. Dr. Pollock must be a very able man. He is a Knight Commander of the Royal Victorian Order and a Doctor of Divinity. He lives in a Palace, sits in the House of Lords and draws a salary of over £4,000 a year. In return for all this, as a minister of religion, he should at least be able to give some definite information about the after-life to those in need of comfort. What good is religion if it cannot ease a soul's distress? If Dr. Pollock had been in that shop when the grief-stricken mother broke down, what would he have said to her? Presumably, he would have told her—"Have faith; we hope that some day you and your son will meet again, but it is not God's will that you should know anything about it."

The Spiritualist who, by directing the mother to a Spiritualist church, brought to her comfort and the knowledge that her son was not "dead," was the Good Samaritan in the case. She did something worth while. And in doing so she performed a far finer act of service than the mere repetition of platitudinous phrases which most people already know by heart. Can any intelligent person truthfully say that homilies on faith and hope are "something better" than the definite knowledge which soothed this woman's heart and eased her sorrow?

It is extraordinary how this over-worked phrase, " The will of God," is used as an explanation of all sorts of occurrences and on all sorts of occasions. If an earthquake wipes out a city it is said to be " The will of God." If anyone is killed by lightning it is " The will of God." God is made responsible for every catastrophe that takes place ; in fact, the phrase is continually used by many people as a kind of mental trench in which they can duck their heads whenever trouble is around.

On the day war broke out in 1939 the then Archbishop of Canterbury, Dr. Lang, broadcast to the country that the outbreak of hostilities was " God's will." What a blasphemous assertion ! It is astounding that any church leader should make such a statement. This was followed by the Moderator of the General Assembly of the Church of Scotland saying " God's purpose has been to humble our nation to the utmost and to bring it down almost to the dust, so that it might be brought to see the peril of its ways." And, not to be outdone in the public expression of such sentiments, the Rev. A. McLeod, speaking in the Glasgow Presbytery of the Free Church of Scotland, exclaimed " We realise that behind these things is the hand of God, and that Hitler and his associates are but the rods in His hands to chastise the nations."

Now, what can the man in the street think of statements such as these ? Whatever may be the faults of our nation, or of others, can he be expected to believe that the cold and premeditated blood-lust of Hitler and his thugs, which has caused sorrow and misery to tens of millions of human beings, was really the "purpose of God," and that He deliberately used these men to "chastise the nations" by means of every ghastly bestiality the mind of man can conceive?

What a conception of God!

To me it seemed incomprehensible until, by chance, I read a review of a book, "The Bible of the World," by the Very Rev. Dr. Matthews, Dean of St. Paul's. Then I understood. Although I must confess that, knowing Dr. Matthews's interest in Spiritualism, I was grieved to find that he had allowed his clerical training to overcome his spiritual convictions. Because, in his review, he denied that there could be such a thing as a universal Bible, and he based this assertion on the fact that "the God of the Hebrews and of the Christians still remains a jealous God." That short sentence caught my attenton. It made me think of the god (to spell the word with a capital G savours almost of irreverence) we read of in the early books of the Bible—an angry, jealous god who meted out death and destruction whenever it pleased him to do so. But, strictly speaking, Dr. Matthews was right. The god of the Hebrews *is* the God of the Christians, although I imagine that few Christians will be pleased at being reminded of the fact! A god who was once capable of drowning the entire population of the world, simply because they displeased him, is equally capable of using Hitler and his subordinates to slaughter a few million Jews for the same reason.

On a certain occasion, we are told, the Hebrews wanted to march through the land of a neighbouring tribe, the Amalekites, just as Hitler and his henchmen wanted to march through most of Europe. Listen to the "orders of the day" given by this god of the Hebrews, who appears to have been the Commander-in-Chief of the Hebrew armies, to his General in charge of this operation, General Saul :— " Go and smite Amalek, and utterly destroy all that they have, and spare them not ; but slay both man and woman, infant and suckling, ox and sheep, camel and ass." Precisely similar orders were issued by Hitler and carried out to the letter by his subordinates. Now we understand why ! How often during the past six years has the cry gone up to heaven "Why does God allow all this suffering ? " Our church leaders have supplied the answer. Hitler and his associates were " the rods in His hands to chastise the nations." The whole ghastly business was " God's will " and part of " God's purpose " in dealing with the human race ! Can any intelligent person believe it ? No wonder the churches are emptying and the " drift from religion " grows steadily from year to year.

But is there a drift from religion ? I do not think so. There is certainly a drift from the doctrines of orthodoxy, but not from religion which is something very different. " Christ attracts," said Dr. Lang some years ago, " but the Church repels." On the other hand the Secretary of the Inter-Denominational Committee of Clergy has stated " There never was a time of such deep longing for evidence of spiritual realities as there is to-day."

Spiritualism is based on " spiritual realities." The place to look for such realities is not necessarily in the Divinity Schools of our Universities. They may certainly be found there, as elsewhere, but that is not because of the theological teaching they impart but rather in spite of it. Spirituality springs from the heart, not from the head. It is not bounded by creeds or doctrines, or by a knowledge of Latin, Greek or Hebrew. It does not belong to one religion more than to another. Mr. Oaten, whose name I have already mentioned in this chapter, once suggested to Dr. Temple, when he was Archbishop of York, that in order to promote brotherhood and toleration amongst the peoples of the world, a World Congress of Faiths might be called with a view to discovering—not the differences between them—but the basic principles on which all were agreed. Dr. Temple replied that " under no circumstances could a Christian consent to meet representatives of other religions on equal terms." Since he made that statement Dr. Temple has passed to the other side of life. It is interesting to speculate in what particularly exclusive circle of society he is now moving in the Spirit World. Perhaps by this time he has changed his opinions. For his own sake, I hope so.

This reminds me of the amusing story of the Roman Catholic prelate who died and was ushered through the pearly gates by St. Peter. He demanded to be taken immediately into the presence of God. After ascending several golden staircases he at last found himself in the Holy of Holies. Seated on sundry thrones were a number of his clerical friends who had predeceased him. After nodding to them a friendly greeting he caught sight of a

crowd of people standing some little distance away.
" Who are these ? " he asked St. Peter.   " Oh,
you needn't worry about them," was the response,
" they are only Church of England folk ; they
never come too near."   " Of course, naturally,"
replied the prelate, and then, as his eyes ranged
further afield, he noticed a dense but indistinct
mass of humanity almost on the edge of the
horizon.   " And who are these—outside—over
there ? " he inquired.   " These ? "   answered
Peter, " Why, these are the Spiritualists ; they
are the only people God does not need to keep His
eye on."   Perhaps, after all, there is some
justification for the belief that the faithful spend
eternity gathered closely round the Throne !

I cannot claim originality for this story, but in
fairness to all concerned I must qualify it by adding
that it was first told me by a member of the Church
of Scotland.   It was therefore only natural that the
favoured and distant host were not Spiritualists
but Presbyterians !

Jesus of Nazareth never attained to any high
rank as a dignitary of the church. He never received
the degree of Doctor of Divinity or Doctor of Laws.
He never professed to be more than a humble Jew,
the son of a carpenter.   He did not live in a palace
or receive a salary of several thousands of year for
teaching His simple beliefs.   In many respects He
was not what some people would call a " religious "
man, as He poured contempt upon the orthodoxy
of His day and mercilessly exposed the hollowness
of forms and ceremonies.   But withal, He was
the greatest and grandest example of spiritual

realities the world has ever known. The world was
His church and humanity His brethren.

To-day, many people have put their Bibles on
the shelf and have almost forgotten their existence,
because they cannot believe the stories it contains
about His life and works. His "miracles," so
called, are beyond their comprehension and are
consequently dismissed as impossible fairy tales.
But they, too, were spiritual realities. And not
only the gospels but the whole Bible, from cover to
cover, is full of these realities. A clergyman once
asked me if I believed that Jesus actually appeared
to Paul on the road to Damascus. When I replied
that I saw no reason to doubt the fact, he seemed
surprised and said that, in his opinion, the story
was merely an example of Eastern symbolism !

Such an occurrence was beyond that man's
understanding. It seemed impossible. But to
one who himself has seen a spirit form and heard
him speak, or who has heard a medium describe the
spirit people, giving names and messages from
them which prove their identity, that vivid story
of Paul's clairvoyance and clairaudience presents
no such difficulties. The same applies to the story
of the appearance of Moses and Elias on the Mount
of Transfiguration. If these things happen to-day,
as I have endeavoured to demonstrate in these
pages, there is no valid reason why they should
not also have happened nineteen hundred years ago.
Similarly, if they happened nineteen hundred years
ago there is no valid reason why they should not
happen to-day. Spiritual realities do not change.
Jesus healed the sick by the power of spirit. So

did His disciples and many members of the early Christian church. The same power heals the sick to-day. Thousands of Spiritualists can testify to this " miracle " in modern life. I have not only seen it done ; I have experienced it myself.

Throughout the ages of history " the gifts of the spirit " have been the channel for the communication of God's teaching to the human race. Without these gifts there can be no revelation. Spiritualism embraces the study of the science of communication with the Spirit World. It teaches that spiritual laws operate throughout the universe and are applicable to all, both here and hereafter, irrespective of colour, country or creed. It asserts that knowledge and instruction are obtainable from higher spheres, by which every soul may be helped to play his part worthily on the stage of life. To a distracted and materialistic world Spiritualism has come to show that mankind is not left to struggle alone against the problems and difficulties which surround him, but that, in very truth, God has " given His angels charge over us," so that we may be helped by stronger forces than our own and guided by those of greater wisdom.

We read that when Philip found Nathaniel he said to him " We have found him of whom Moses and the Law and the Prophets did write, Jesus of Nazareth, the son of Joseph." Nathaniel answered " Can any good thing come out of Nazareth ? " Philip said to him " Come and see." He came and was convinced of the truth of what Philip had told him.

To-day, Spiritualism would guide a troubled world to the source from which all the great teachers of the past received their inspiration, the seers and prophets their vision and their power. It would bring to the sad and lonely both knowledge and comfort, to the leaders of the nations a wisdom beyond human understanding. To this the world replies " Can any good come out of Spiritualism ? " We can only say, like Philip, " Come and see." And those who come in singleness of purpose and with a sincere desire to learn will assuredly find their coming has not been in vain.

Kilmarnock:
THE "STANDARD" PRESS.
1946.